One Loving Life Is All There Is

Mary Woods

Published by Mary Woods, 2023.

ONE LOVING LIFE IS ALL THERE IS

First edition. February 3, 2023.

Written by Mary Woods.

Table of Contents

Preface: The Timeline of One Loving Life

"Live for yourself, live for life, then you are truly a friend of man." ~Kahlil Gibran

Life is eternal and one loving life is all there is. Our purpose is to be the light of the world, forgive our illusions, and express love in our own unique, creative ways. Life is our piece of art. Appreciating the gift of our life, experiencing being human, a human being, is enough. Life can be simple.

Our ego identification can make life complicated. We judge ourselves as not good enough, that we don't do enough, and that we don't have enough. The ego always compares itself to others, competes with, or wants approval from others. The ego feels obligated, pressured, and makes many demands of what it needs and 'should' do.

Our Higher Self is content to 'just be'. We can tell our ego, "enough is enough!" We are absolutely enough. We are a child of God with an eternal divine soul, having a temporary human experience. We are here to express love, which is what we are.

As we learn to stay in the present moment, in the eternal now, we can experience the timelessness of the holy instant. Looking at the timeline of our human lifetime with the Holy Spirit, allows us to keep all that is good and true from our past, while forgiving and releasing all the rest.

We can perceive our own story as a hologram of projection and as our classroom in lessons of love and forgiveness. We can look at the stories of our generation in time together, to remember and re-evaluate our shared collective experiences. To share the innocent perception of one loving life, allows the ego to be undone, and with it, all fear and guilt, so we can remember Who We Are, by identifying with the Truth of our Being.

> "All your past except its beauty is gone, and nothing is left but a blessing. I have saved all your kindnesses and every loving thought you ever had. I have purified them of the errors that hid their light, and kept them for you in perfect radiance. They are beyond destruction and beyond guilt. They came from the Holy Spirit within you, and we know that what God Creates is eternal." ~A Course In Miracles T.5- IV. 8: 2-6

There are many ideas about alternative timelines for humanity's future. Yet, if we trust in God, our loving Creator, we can be assured that "God's Will be done on earth as it is in Heaven." We are all part of life and since God is all Life, we are all part of God. We can have faith in our positive timeline because *we are* the positive timeline. We share one loving life in time and eternity.

One lifetime timeline is archetypal of both our culture and the counter culture of the day. 'Her'-story is relevant to our common experiences of the current events of the time, with our collective purpose of raising the consciousness of humanity. Each decade shares a journey in our One Loving Life;

A Baby Boomer born in the 1950's
A Flower Child in the 1960's
The Culture of Sex, Drugs, and Rock 'n Roll in the 1970's
On Spiritual Sabbatical in the 1980's
Working in Spiritual Communities in the 1990's
A Holistic Educator in the 2000's

A Practical Mystic in the 2010's
A Spiritual Warrior in the 2020's

Introduction

"An unexamined life is not worth living." ~Socrates

Do you remember the 'reality' television show, "This Is Your Life," hosted by Ralph Edwards, that originated in the 1950's? Filmed in front of a 'live' audience, the host took special guests through a retrospective of their lives, with surprise appearances from family, friends, and colleagues, to commemorate their life accomplishments and appreciation for the memories they shared.

It was one of those early childhood memories of the 'programs' that came into our living room through the black and white TV set. My parents told me that after I learned to say, "MaMa" and "DaDa," that "Perry Como" was one of my first spoken words. Our family would ritually gather around our TV set in the evenings to tune into those entertainment programs, along with millions of others in the collective consciousness, we went along with the program.

In retrospect, could our innocent perception of those family entertainment shows really be a form of mind 'entrainment'? From our current perspective, we have a disclosure of a lifelong agenda of the global elite for mind control, mass hypnosis, and programmed propaganda that has been systematically used to manipulate the mass population into a false narrative. The social engineering of our reality has been a contrived program of our minds, from watching programs on television, to getting with the program in society.

It is my intention to show how our generation has been the product of this social engineering experiment throughout our lives; within our educational systems, religious systems, political systems, medical systems, environmental controls, genetically modified foods, advertising, the cultural norms of television programs, Hollywood movies, popular music, sexual identity programs, and on and on, across the board of our 'reality'.

We have been programmed to perceive an inverted reality, an upside down perception, where what is good becomes bad and what is bad becomes good; the innocent are guilty and the guilty are innocent. Disinformation, misinformation, fake news, propaganda in the mainstream media; How can anyone discern what is real and what is really going on?

In my opinion, exposing and disclosing the lies is a necessary step in deprogramming the population, so that the truth will be revealed. It is like the prophetic, biblical "apocalypse," which means the lifting of the veil from what has been happening behind the scenes.

"For nothing is secret that will not be revealed. Nor anything hidden that will not be known and come to light." ~Luke 8:17

Our task, should we choose to accept it, is to bring our personal and collective darkness to the light. In the spotlight of looking at the dark secrets and hidden agendas, they can be exposed and expelled, revealed and healed. As we blow the cover off the deception, like good detectives and conspiracy observers, it will lose the ability to hurt us.

"The journey that we undertake together is the exchange of dark for light, of ignorance for understanding. Nothing you understand is fearful. It is only in darkness and in ignorance that you perceive the frightening, and shrink away from it to further darkness. And yet, it is only the hidden that can terrify, not for what it is, but for its hiddenness." ~A Course In Miracles T.14. VI. 1-4

We the People can be empowered to wake up from the mass hypnosis and take back our power from the 'power over' agenda. As we awaken from the deep hypnotic trance of separation, we will experience a 'trance-formation' into unity consciousness because we are all one and all in this together.

Who Are We? Remember the theme song of our Woodstock generation;

"We are stardust. We are golden. We are caught in the devil's bargain. And we've got to get ourselves back to the garden." ~Joni Mitchell

We live in a time of prophecy as the Hopi Elders declared;

"We Are The Ones We've Been Waiting For."

Instead of waiting for someone to rescue us or do it for us, we can choose to wake up from our sleep of forgetfulness and remember Who We Are. It is my passion and calling to wake people up to the Truth of our Being, to dream a new dream, before we awaken from the dream altogether.

This is my story of one loving life. It is also our story, since we are all here together, at the same time. We have the power to change the way we look at life, to understand our higher purpose, and align with The Divine, to co-create this new vision. We are all on the collective Hero's Journey to overcome our obstacles and tell a new story.

How many times have we reiterated, "It's the story of my life" to describe the same old, self-defeating patterns, that we feel hopeless to change and doomed to repeat. Before we can really let go of our old story, we have to begin to allow it, accept it, and appreciate the lessons it has provided for our soul growth. We all have the lesson of learning to love ourselves and our stories, unconditionally.

Telling our life story is relevant now because it is archetypal of the culture of our times. The adage that it is both a blessing and a curse to be born in interesting times relates to our human experience of the best of times and the worst of times. To be born at the end of one age and the birth of a new one reflects the radical and transformational changes inherent in a quantum leap in consciousness.

The surreal, unbelievable, and twilight zone nature of life in our generation, has coined the term, 'you can't make this stuff up'. Yet, if we do make our own reality, we are indeed responsible for what we see and the dream we are dreaming. If truth is stranger than fiction, then our goal for truth leads us to lessons of discernment of the true from the false, the real from the fake, and what is valuable from the valueless.

The paradox of this dualistic world is the two sides of the coin scenario. With different perspectives, everyone sees things differently, and the 'truth' seems to become a relative perception. Yet, if we could be willing to look at the way things really are in our world, as well as, have the goal of the absolute Truth with a capitol T, that transcends our limited perceptions, we could lift above the battlefield into the Truth of our Oneness.

At the time of this writing, the internet platform "Truth Social" is just coming online. Presented as a means for free speech without censorship, it is intended to be a voice for the people. Are we willing to look at the 'truth' of social engineering? Can we look at it together, without judgment, with a willingness to heal and release the past? Can we change our minds about Who We Are, and begin to co-create the new paradigm as free, conscious, sovereign beings? Like imaginal cells in the chrysalis, lets imagine the possibilities that can heal and transform our world.

"There are no limitations unless you create them yourselves. Anything is possible. You are only limited by your own imagination." ~Nikola Tesla

A Baby Boomer From The 1950's

"You are a child of the universe no less than the trees and the stars; you have a right to be here. And whether or not it is clear to you, no doubt the universe is unfolding as it should." ~from Desiderata

In 1956, the year of my birth, Eisenhower was President, and Elvis Presley was King. It was the middle of the Baby Boom, which began in 1946, the year my sister was born. After World War II ended, the generation of Baby Boomers populated the planet from 1946-1964.

The American Dream of capitalism, free enterprise, and economic growth was also having a boom. Our parents had survived the Great Depression and a World War, and were motivated to live a peaceful, prosperous, good life. Patriotism, commercialism, and optimism were strong in the 'Father Knows Best' world of the 1950's.

We were told that the Nuremberg Trials and Code would prevent the crimes against humanity that occurred in Nazi Germany from ever happening again. We were not told, however, that 1500 top Nazi Scientists moved to America after the war to seed the Military Industrial Complex, in a CIA project known as 'Operation Paperclip'. Was this the beginning of an ideological contamination and infiltration of our country?

Wernon Von Braun and his team of rocket scientists were instrumental in NASA's development of weapons in space. Other Nazi scientists experimented with LSD, MK Ultra, and other mind control programs. We, the American public, were unknowingly the test subjects of secret programs that infiltrated our government, our media, and our culture in far-reaching ways. Did we really win World War II or were we infiltrated, instead of invaded, by weapons of social engineering?

President Eisenhower warned us about the dangers of secret societies and the rise of the Military Industrial Complex, as did President Kennedy in the next decade. The term "conspiracy theorist" arose in the 1950's, as an insult and stigmatized label for anyone questioning the official narrative. There is evidence to suggest that the CIA invented the term to make a mockery of anyone who was suspicious about UFO cover-ups or other hidden agendas. We were socially engineered to protect the established doctrine by judging those that did not conform as kooks, nutcases, heretics, or conspiracy theorists.

This was the state of affairs in our world when the Baby Boomers arrived, with our soul contract for a lifetime. Our eternal, divine soul came in with universal, unalienable rights to freely create our own reality, or was our freedom co-opted from the beginning? Were we born into a conspiracy with a 'big steal agenda' that asked, how can we trap a soul's lifetime into our system? How can they be used to make money for us?

A scheme was developed to issue a birth certificate, along with income tax, to entrap a soul's lifetime. Each birth certificate would have a number that was associated with a bond. The bond represented a projection into the future of each soul's financial value. Did you know that the US government has been trading these bonds on Wall St? They are betting on how much money we will make in our lifetime. The bond certificate is based on our financial net worth. That is why we are required to earn money and pay taxes to fund the bond. Are we actually bonded as economic slaves?

Along with our birth certificate, we had our records of childhood vaccinations. Not only were we indoctrinated into the economic system, but the medical system as well. Those injections were necessary for our entrance into the educational system, all which reinforced following the rules, obeying the authorities, and doing what you are told. We would be punished if we got out of line. We were taught to conform to the norm.

Maybe some of our generation incarnated to be system busters, or part of the counter-culture during the hippie movement, that coined the slogan, "Question Authority." The retrospective journey of our lives illustrates how we responded, survived, and even thrived during the current events of our times. We had clues all of our lives about our soul purpose to raise the consciousness of humanity; to be optimistic, keep the faith, and trust that things always work out. We were often accused of seeing the world through rose colored glasses, with a Pollyanna perspective, and in denial about the dark side.

It must have been our invincible spirit, combined with an innate innocence, that gave us such a hopeful attitude. Yet it was my destiny written within my astrological birth chart, (north node in Scorpio in the 8th house), that always showed me the hidden darkness within my ego and in the ego's world. My spiritual path of *A Course In Miracles* taught;

"No one can escape from illusions unless he looks at them, for not looking is the way they are protected." ~T.11. V:1

I don't remember much of the 1950's because my birthday is December 29, 1956. My entry into the world included an initial birth trauma of being a breech baby with the umbilical cord choking my neck. Since the doctors and nurses had to give me mouth-to-mouth resuscitation to get me to breathe, my life began with a near death experience. In retrospect, it may have been an appropriate metaphor to explain my upside down perception and the strangle hold on my throat to keep me from speaking my truth. Yet, that is another story from the past, which has all been forgiven and healed now.

My arrival was a real surprise for my parents, who had me at 40 years old, along with my much older two brothers, ages 19 and 15 and my two sisters, ages 14 and 10. Christened Mary Margaret, I was named Mary after my four Great-Grandmothers and Margaret after my Mother's Sister. My family tell many stories about how I was the center of attention, had several nicknames, and was both well-loved and loving. What a blessing to have such a big family and surrounded by love.

I still have my first Teddy Bear, who like the Velveteen Rabbit, has been loved so hard that it became 'Real'. He is thread bare and worn, but it just makes him more endearing. His companion is my doll Lolly Pink, with the Mona Lisa smile, who is in a perpetual state of bliss. Both serve to remind me of my inner child, who is still alive and well.

A Flower Child of the 1960's

"Maybe it's the time of year, or maybe it's the time of man. I don't know who I am, but life is for learning." ~Joni Mitchell from "Woodstock"

It was a decade of transformational and revolutionary change, both personally and collectively. Growing up as a child in the culture of the 1960's had a major influence on our lives during these formative years. Archetypal of the Magical/Mystical/Innocent Child, gifted with the belief that anything was possible, the qualities of lightheartedness and purity of soul are still our greatest gifts.

The music of the 60's was legendary. Songs play in our memories like the soundtrack of the movie of our life and we can't overestimate the influence they impressed upon our minds. From following the bouncing ball as we were entrained to "Sing Along With Mitch," to the good ol' days of rock and roll, we would dance along with the Dick Clark Show, doing the jitterbug, the slide, the swim, and "come on everybody, let's do the twist." The early 60's music plays like the Wolfman Jack radio program from American Graffiti. Chuck Berry, Dion, Trini Lopez, The Everley Brothers, Roy Orbison, Chubby Checker, Jan and Dean, The Beach Boys, and The Token's one hit wonder, "The Lion Sleeps Tonight."

The party of our childhood was interrupted the day our second grade class was sent home from school with news that President Kennedy had been shot and killed. My mother and grandmother were crying in front of our black and white TV set. How could this happen? Mom said there are bad people in the world that do bad things. Our nation mourned as we watched Jackie Kennedy in her black veil and Little John John saluting his Father's coffin in the funeral procession. In retrospect, it was my first observation of a conspiracy, November 1963.

A few months later in 1964, was the memorable night that The Beatles were on "The Ed Sullivan Show". Again, it was through the portal of our black and white TV set, that the 'British Invasion' came into our living room. My teenage sister was screaming along with the TV audience of young women who were dramatically overcome by these four long-haired boys singing and playing guitars. Our parents were seriously concerned that something was wrong here. After The Beatles arrived on the scene, the soundtrack changed, as the message music of the hippie movement started to engage our minds.

1965 was a turning point. All of my brothers and sisters moved out of our house that year; Fred got married, Richard got an apartment, Michele got married, and Karen went away to college. Fortunately, my new best friend moved into the house next door that same year. Lisa and I were very imaginative with our playtime game of "lets pretend." We would set up furniture to create spaces in our basement to play house, store, office, restaurant, doctor, and to put on talent shows for our parents. We played board games like Monopoly, Scrabble, Life, Careers, Park & Shop, Password, Operation, Risk, Mouse Trap, and card games like Rummy, War, Go Fish, Crazy 8's, Old Maid, Pitch, and Poker.

We rode our bicycles around the neighborhood, walked on sidewalks and nature trails, played fort, hide and seek, step school, bad mitten, and street games like Tag, Mother May I, and Red Light. In the warm weather, we could stay outside till dark, collecting lightning bugs in a jar with holes punched in the lid. We loved to be in the sun and in the water, from our little plastic pool in our backyard to our neighborhood swimming pool. We could run fast, keep the hula hoop up for a long time, and climb up high into the branches of trees to hide under the leaves so no one could find us.

As a child of the 60's, we were definitely into television programs. Our education began with "Romper Room" and Miss Nancy's teaching of the "DoBe." We can still sing from memory both the jingles of the commercials and the theme songs of our favorite shows. Remember the tune, "You'll look better in a sweater washed in Woolite. Woolite makes a sweater look alive!"

and the sound of, "Snap, Crackle, Pop, Rice Krispies." To show how much we were programmed, bet you still know the words to the songs from, "Gilligan's Island," "The Beverly Hillbillies," "The Flintstones," "Spiderman," "The Jetsons," "The Monkeys," "Secret Agent Man," and the musical tracks from "The Twilight Zone," "Leave It To Beaver," Dennis the Menace," "Bewitched," "Lassie," and dozens of others.

The sound of "Walt Disney's Wonderful World of Color" on our new color TV set, that came on Sunday night, was always a reminder that the next day was a school day. Disney shows were supposed to be so wholesome with morals to the stories. *Fantasia, Cinderella, Sleeping Beauty, Peter Pan,* and *Snow White,* and all the fairy tales we were told. Little did we know the deeper meaning of the idea that it was all a world of make believe. The disclosure that Walt Disney was a 33rd degree mason, deeply entrenched with the Nazis in mind control programming, sexual deviation, with underground tunnels at Disneyland, allegedly for child trafficking, was not known to me at the time. The point is, we were all going along with the program of the conspiracy disguised as a children's show, not knowing it was a wolf in sheep's clothing.

The second half of the 60's decade gained momentum with revolutionary changes. The cover of Time magazine asked, "Is God Dead?" in 1966. The Beatles album, "The Magical Mystery Tour" came out in 1967, with the album played on a different speed to reveal the words, "I bury Paul," fueling the conspiracy that the real Paul McCartney died in a car accident and was replaced by a look alike double. The radical year of 1968 televised the blatant conspiracies in the murders of Martin Luther King and Bobby Kennedy, along with the deaths of more of our soldiers in Vietnam.

While the ideals of peace and love were trying to be the answer, we were also dealing with the conflicts of war and fear that were an escalating problem in our world. The Gulf of Tonkin event that got America into the Vietnam war is now known to have been an engineered false flag, ironically involving Jim Morrison's father, Admiral George Morrison. Martin Luther King, Jr. had become one of the country's most prominent opponents of the war and an outspoken critic of overall U.S. foreign policy. Bobby Kennedy, as the District Attorney, was going after the mafia and criminal networks that were actively working with the U.S. government. The power of these two leaders of the people was seen as a threat to the powers that valued war to improve the economy and other selfish agendas.

It was also the time of the Women's Liberation Movement, with bra burning and the sexual revolution encouraged by the birth control pill. The conspiracy was that Gloria Steinhem and Ms. Magazine were undercover CIA agents with the agenda to get women into the working world in order to make more tax money, buy more things, and break up the family. We were oblivious to all this propaganda at the time, as we saw Gloria and Betty Fredan as role models for women's lib; equal pay for women, setting women free from stereotypes, and legalizing abortion.

It was a significant and impressionable time during my 12th year in 1969. Receiving my Confirmation into the Catholic Church, identifying as a 'Jesus Freak', attending prayer meetings called, "Young Life," and getting spiritually high on my love for God and Jesus. Also identifying as a Flower Child, wearing wildflower clovers made into a chain in my long hair, that I loved to wash with Herbal Essence shampoo. The popular photograph in Life magazine of a little girl putting a daisy in the tip of a Vietnam soldier's gun, expressed my sentiments exactly. We were all about flower power, the peace sign, and the slogan "make love not war."

1969 was also the year of Woodstock, the rock festival of our generation, and my sister Karen was there. We all felt that we were part of a movement of "Peace, Love, and Music" and "a cog in something turning," that reflected a big change in our collective consciousness. Bob Dylan had foretold, "The Times they are A Changin;" Crosby, Stills, Nash, and Young advised us to "Teach Your Children (and parents) Well;" and The Youngbloods inspired us to, "Come on people now, smile on your brother, everybody get together and try to love one another right now."

We took the message music to heart. We graduated from 45's to albums, from bubblegum to heavy rock. Listening to The Doors, The Moody Blues, Jefferson Airplane, Janice Joplin, Jimi Hendrix, Procol Harum, Steppenwolf, The Byrds, The Who, Donovan; We got the message from The Fifth Dimension that it was "the Dawning of the Age of Aquarius" and from The Beatles that, "All You Need Is Love."

What we didn't know at the time, was that the 1960's counter-culture movement was a covert operation directed by the CIA. From its development during the Cold War, the Central Intelligence Agency co-opted the news media, politics, arts and entertainment, education, spirituality, and cultural norms with propaganda through Operation Mockingbird. The far-reaching extent of manipulation is staggeringly mind- blowing.

One of the CIA's 'think tanks' known as the Tavistock Institute of Human Relations, in cahoots with the Stanford Research Center, were the social engineers targeting the American youth, through their creation of "The Beatles." With the use of atonal sounds in their new kind of "music," combined with heavy media promotion, their mind control experiment was successful in making us think that this was our new favorite band.

Then the newly created music scene moved to Laurel Canyon in the suburbs of LA, CA. In the book, *Weird Scenes Inside The Canyon: Laurel Canyon, Covert Ops, and the Dark Heart of the Hippie Dream*, author David McGowan tells the behind the scenes story. Originating at the military base, "Lookout Mountain Observatory," new music bands were created by the CIA, driven by the children of high ranking military families. While studio bands actually produced the records, we were made to idolize these new 'rock stars', as part of this covert operation, that was the driving force behind the counter culture.

It is with deepest sadness and shock to disclose some of the bands, (most are in my album collection) that David McGowan reveals were CIA engineered in Laurel Canyon; Crosby, Stills Nash; Neil Young, The Doors, The Byrds, The Beach Boys, Poco, America, Buffalo Springfield, Three Dog Night, The Mamas and The Papas; and Frank Zappa, who lived in Laurel Canyon, was the son of a military official, and was a sort of ring leader for CIA operations. There was the intentional use of Satanic music rituals to cast spells on the public.

Magicians wands were often made out of wood from a holly tree, which is the origin of the name, "Hollywood;" a global programming operation. Many actors in Hollywood and the singers in the music industry are under trauma-based mind control to serve the mass perception-programming agenda. Many stage shows, videos, music, and movies feature blatant Satanic and secret society rituals, projecting visual and audio frequencies to put a spell on the minds of the audience.

A series of night clubs in LA created hippie dancers to demonstrate the new scene of psychedelic rock. In San Francisco's Haight Ashbury, groups like the Grateful Dead and Jefferson Airplane were promoting drugs like LSD, which was developed by the CIA to study how to control people. Ken Kesey and The Merry Pranksters were test subjects of the CIA's notorious MKUltra Program, promoting 'acid trips' as part of the music scene.

Professor Timothy O'Leary from Harvard University worked with the CIA to normalize LSD, with his slogan, "Turn On, Tune In, Drop Out." Getting kids hooked on "Sex, Drugs, and Rock 'n Roll" was a distraction from the anti-war protests and the revolution that was in process. The protesters were made to look like drugged out hippies, instead of conscientious Americans attempting to overthrow the military industrial complex.

"We'll know our disinformation program is complete when everything the American public believes is false." ~William Casey, CIA Director

The Culture of Sex, Drugs, and Rock & Roll in the 1970's

"I don't believe people are looking for the meaning of life as much as they are looking for the experience of being alive." ~Joseph Campbell

The 1970's have been called the decade of decadence. It began with the shock of the killing of four students protesting the Vietnam War on the campus of Kent State University by the Ohio National Guard. That same month, May 1970, I was the first sign of violence in a racial riot in downtown Baltimore. I had cut school with two friends from my neighborhood to attend the annual Flower Mart event. As we were walking around, I was suddenly accosted by a black woman who was trying to steal my purse. While we were engaged in a tug of war, a black man punched me in the face with brass knuckles. The next thing I remember was being helped up by an elderly black woman, who waited until my friends found me. Danny had been punched in the jaw and Brian had been spared, yet we realized that we had better leave the scene quickly, so we headed to the nearby hospital. While we were in the waiting room, we saw stretcher after stretcher of women brought in who were clearly worse off than us.

The x-rays showed that Danny had a broken jaw and I had a broken nose and a black eye that was swollen shut. Still in shock, my biggest concern was 'getting grounded' as punishment from my parents. I was out of commission and school for two weeks with a white patch over my eye. The worst part was the pain of getting my nose fixed, but we were grateful that everything healed and grateful that we weren't dead.

The social and political strife of the time provided fertile ground for the counterculture to emerge. Not since the Civil war had our country been so divided. Our generation coined the meme, "don't trust anyone over 30," as we managed to expose the facade of the establishment and the hypocrisies beneath the apparent social order.

Our parents felt the contentions of this 'generation gap' that tried to put a wedge between us. Yet my parents were not strangers to accepting differences, in that my Mother was a Catholic Democrat and my Father was an Agnostic Republican. My Mother demonstrated the Mother Theresa archetype of selfless service to others, while my Father was an advocate of the Ayn Rand philosophy of *The Virtue of Selfishness*. This led to many lively discussions around the dinner table as we had healthy debates and equally shared perspectives of 'both sides now'.

In 1970, my father was reading the prophetic bestseller, *Future Shock* by Alvin Toffler, about the coming exponential changes and their radical effects on society. Life really did pick up speed with so many changes, both personally and collectively. My sister and brother-in-law got married and moved away that year. We were told that Jimi Hendrix and Janis Joplin died from drug overdoses, along with Jim Morrison the next year.

Nixon was president and we watched the Watergate scandal unfold as another conspiracy of political corruption. The trials were televised and seemed to go on forever, illustrating the controversy and controlling agendas in government. Frank Zappa commented on the narrative by saying, "Politics is the entertainment division of the military industrial complex."

A popular television show of the 1970's was "All In The Family," with Archie and Edith representing our parents generation, reminiscing about more simple times in their theme song, "Those Were The Days." The disclosure film of *The Network* exposed the manipulation of the media in the news anchor Howard Beale's famous speech,

"Television is not the truth. Television is a god-damn amusement park. You do what the tube tells you. You people are the real thing. We are the illusion. Turn off your TV. I want you to stand up and yell, "I'm mad as hell and I'm not going to take it anymore.""

My social life was blooming into the teenage years of 'the dating game'. It was a fun way to get out of the house and go to the movies, dances, concerts, carnivals, fairs, amusement parks, bowling, miniature golf, and restaurants. It was customary to 'go steady' or date just one boy at a time, and your boyfriend would give you his I.D. Bracelet. The dates would usually culminate with a 'make- out' session, where the guys would see how far they could get around 'the bases'. When things would start to get hot and heavy, my mantra, "I am going to stay a virgin until I am married" would bring the session to a halt. With sex definitely not an option, we would soon 'break up', and just date someone else.

In retrospect, these dating rituals were an example of social engineering. The goal of dating, for many guys, was to 'go all the way'. Girls who 'put out' would quickly get a 'reputation' or get pregnant, so they had more to lose in the game. Into this age-old program, came the birth control pill, giving birth to the sexual revolution! Sex was suddenly encouraged, expected, and engineered into the culture of "free love." Sex education was being taught in school. We were exposed to socially acceptable pornography in R an X rated movies, Playboy and Penthouse magazines, subliminal advertising, and sexual innuendo in language, clothing, and behavioral conditioning.

It has been said that "if you remember the 1970's, then you weren't there," implying that if you were there, you were stoned, high, or under the influence of mind altering drugs. Passing 'joints' of pot, weed, or marijuana was commonplace in many social settings. Smoking pot was not only a ritual at most parties, but was actively used and available from students in our 'high' school. My college had a popular club called the International Bonging

Association, where we would smoke pot out of 'bongs' and water pipes. While it was socially acceptable, it was also illegal, which led to the fear of getting 'busted' and the paranoia of 'narcs', a narcotic police officer in disguise. My college boyfriend got busted for selling marijuana to a narc that he knew as an old friend, and was sent to a drug rehabilitation program.

Although pot was not dangerous or addictive, it was often an entry into the drug culture. There were just so many ways to "get high;" hashish, hash oil, cocaine, speed in the form of amphetamines, downers in the form of qualudes, LSD in the form of Mr. Natural, Windowpane, Orange Sunshine, Ecstasy, and other synthetic LSD. Psilocybin mushrooms, peyote, and ayahuasca are natural forms of "tripping." I have safely experienced some of these, which have usually invoked expanded states of mind and deeper spiritual connections. This was never something I went looking for, but came to me at different times in my life. Although my stories are positive ones, there are many who were damaged by tainted drugs, overdoses, addiction, incarceration, and even loss of life. Drug production, smuggling, and distribution are a huge business and a major instrument of social engineering, mind control, and mass manipulation.

The music industry was a major contributor to making this all socially acceptable and especially "cool." Jimi Hendrix, who was said to have died from an overdose, wrote classic drug songs like, "Are You Experienced" and "Purple Haze;" The Beatles song, "Lucy in the Sky with Diamonds" was code for LSD; Eric Clapton's song "Cocaine;" The Grateful Dead wrote, "Driving that train, high on cocaine, Casey Jones you better watch your speed;" Jefferson Airplane's classic, "One pill makes you larger and one pill makes you small, and the one that Mother gives you, doesn't do anything at all. Go ask Alice when she's ten feet tall;" Little Feat sang, "Don't Bogart that joint, my friend, pass it over to me;" Then Cheech and Chong showed us how to do it.

Did the culture of sex, drugs, and rock and roll corrupt us? For some, yes, but for those of us who survived the decade of decadence, what didn't kill us made us stronger. Many had mind-expanding awareness, creative ideas, and deep philosophical conversations. Spiritual teacher Ram Dass experimented with drugs and said that the problem was that it was a temporary state of mind and then you would come down. He went to India to study with enlightened sages, who taught him how to find that spiritual awakening within himself, without the use of drugs.

My own experience of Spiritual Awakening was without the use of drugs, and yet it was clearly an altered state of higher consciousness. Perceiving the world as an upside down perception, inverted from reality, gave me the recognition, like Master Yoda said, "You must unlearn what you have learned." I was guided from within, to quit college in 1977, which I understood to be an educational indoctrination into a contrived system, and to continue my learning in the School of Life, with the Holy Spirit as my Teacher. It was then that I realized God, our Divine Creator, was available within our own True Self.

"We don't need no education. We don't need no thought control."
~The Wall by Pink Floyd

After graduating with highest honors and a two year Associate Arts degree in Education, my studies continued in more unconventional ways. Philosophy and comparative religions were my favorite subjects. As a spiritual seeker, bookstores and libraries became a favorite place, where I would often experience books falling off the shelf, like an oracle telling me just what I needed to know. Some of the more significant ones were; *Handbook to Higher Consciousness* by Ken Keyes, *The Lazy Man's Guide To Enlightenment* by Thaddeus Golas, *The Magic of Findhorn* by Paul Hawken, *Siddhartha* by Herman Hesse, *The Prophet* by Kahlil Gibran, *There is a River* by Thomas Sugrue and other books about Edgar Cayce.

Since our parents had the belief that "as long as you live in my house, you have to live by our rules," I had moved into my own apartment with a girlfriend in 1976. Relishing in my freedom, I worked at various jobs to cover my expenses; Sears Driving School, The Credit Bureau, Hostess at the Holiday Inn, Child Care for a working couple, and even Telephone Soliciting. It felt good to be responsible, independent, and make my own balanced lifestyle.

I had turned around the decadence of the "sex, drugs, and rock & roll syndrome" by maintaining healthy "serial monogamous" relationships with boyfriends, smoking pot when it would show up and it was appropriate, and enjoying the best of the music of the decade. We all had an album collection, loved to go to concerts, and go out dancing to live music. My favorite bands and songs that played in the soundtrack of my mind; Crosby Stills Nash & Young, Van Morrison, Eagles, James Taylor, Carol King, America, Loggins & Messina, Poco, The Band, Fleetwood Mac, Steeley Dan, Santana, Pink Floyd, Traffic, Linda Ronstadt, Jackson Brown, Little Feat, Doobie Brothers, Allman Brothers.

In March of 1979, when in Ft. Pierce, Florida on a business trip with associates from United Labs of America, I met my future husband. It was like we recognized each other, or was it love at first sight? After he came up to visit me in my apartment, we decided to spend a month together in Puerto Rico, at his favorite surfing spot, which would eventually become our home in the 1980's. Meanwhile, I moved to Ft. Pierce, FL., and shared a house on the beach with a girlfriend, where I worked as a Day Care Teacher, and then, the Art Director for a local newspaper. Life took on the fun in the sun lifestyle with a Jimmy Buffet soundtrack, until I got the tragic news that my Mother was dying.

On Spiritual Sabbatical in the 1980's

"Life is a journey, not a destination." ~Ralph Waldo Emerson

While the 1970's began with a punch in my face, they ended with a punch in my gut, when my sister called to tell me that our Mother was diagnosed with lung cancer that had advanced into the bone. She was given a few months to live. It was late in October 1979, when my world came crashing down with this gut wrenching, heart breaking realization. My heart knew without a doubt that I had to go and be with her.

This meant leaving my promising life in Florida, which included moving from my lovely beach house, quitting my good job, and relocating 1000 miles away from my boyfriend. Yet my heart was sure that being with my Mother in her time of need was more important than anything. Taking her to doctors, radiation and chemo appointments, watching her lose her hair and her life force energy was devastating, but our true love and spiritual strength gave us what we needed most.

Our family Christmas in 1979 was bittersweet and memorable. We all did our best to be upbeat with supportive hugs and laughter, but the gravity of the situation was undeniable. I was with my Mother when she made her transition in February of 1980. This experience was a spiritual gift of love that lives in my heart in words unspoken, though I knew she was with God eternally. In retrospect, my Mother was a woman of God, making her a true Priestess, as she lived a life of devotion and selfless service.

In 1980, our Mother died in February, our Father died in June, and I got married in July. Two funerals and a wedding, marking major life passages as we entered a new decade. Our Father and Mother were born on the same day of the same year, were married 43 years, and it wasn't surprising that they went out so close together. Dad had a cerebral hemorrhage because he had lost his will to live without Mom. It was the end of an era.

Our wedding was symbolic of endings followed by new beginnings. Heartbreak can be heart opening. It was a lovely outdoor ceremony in Florida, another 'celebration of life', full of love, beauty, joy, and hope. We were all making our transition into new territory. Our hearts had been activated, so we followed its lead, trusting it knew the way. Making a commitment to share the journey with my husband opened new vistas for both of us.

We moved into a trailer on a private lot in Ft.Pierce, Florida. We were near my husband's family and friends, as well as the beach, where he frequently went surfing, and I would swim, get tanned, and collect seashells. I found creative employment as a Day Care Teacher on the campus of the local college, along with a part-time waitress job. Just when we were settling down, life brought us more change and transition.

In January of 1981, we returned to Rincon, Puerto Rico, this time to purchase property. With the combination of our savings and my inheritance, we were able to buy an acre of beautiful land on a hill overlooking the Caribbean, just a five minute walk to the beach. It was a popular surfing mecca and a dream-come-true for my husband, who had traveled there often to catch the idyllic island waves.

We rented a small shack close to our land, bought an old car, and began communing with the elements, envisioning our new lifestyle. There were no building codes on the island in those days, so we quickly went about the business of building our own house. We drew out the plans ourselves, bought the pressure treated wood, corrugated zinc for the roof, supplies, and tools, and began constructing our island home.

Local surfers and visiting friends and family came to help us complete our project and within a couple of months we could move in. The house foundation measured 20' x 20', with a 4' porch on two sides. The interior included space for a kitchen, living/dining room, double bed, and a loft bedroom, with an outhouse and shower out the back door. Large open windows with shutters on all four sides made it look spacious.

The front door faced the ocean and the porch included a bench along one side overlooking the valley, with hammocks to enjoy the view. The property already had an avocado tree and a patch of banana trees along the road side of the house, where we built a bamboo walkway entrance. We landscaped with papaya and tropical fruit trees, including a large vegetable garden, and a variety of colorful tropical flowers.

Our house soon became the party place for the other local American surfers, and all those who frequently visited, including our family and friends. People were amazed to see our simple lifestyle in the beautiful natural environment. With a consistent flow of guests, we were often entertaining with food, rum drinks, and homegrown marijuana. Life assumed a laid back, take it easy tempo, with a Bob Marley soundtrack.

In October 1981, we partnered with another local American couple, and opened a health food restaurant that we called, "Punta De Energia" (Energy Point). We rented a space where we set up a kitchen area, built a wooden bar for smoothies and bake goods, and furnished with picnic tables for customers. We had an all vegetarian menu, serving breakfast, lunch, and dinner, 6 days a week.

It was a popular spot for all the surfers, and our claim to fame was a write up in Surfer Magazine with a raving review of our orange walnut pancakes. It was really grueling work, however, to cook full time, daily cleanup, and shopping for supplies on our day off. My husband and I made back the money we invested in the first three months, and after three months of profit, we sold our share of the business, to return to a more simple life.

Our lifestyle and mind set were influenced by the popular books of the day; Reader's Digest, *Back to Basics,* Jethro Klaus', *Back To Eden, The Holistic Health Handbook* by the Berkeley Institute, *The Findhorn Garden,* and various vegetarian cookbooks. The trend was down-to-earth, natural living, making your own products and remedies, growing your own food, eating a vegetarian diet, and communing with nature.

My mind was so expanded by the spiritual books that I was reading, that the 1980's are fondly referred to as my "spiritual sabbatical." After studying the book, *Science and Health* by Mary Baker Eddy, I had the epiphany that, "I Am Spirit." Other major influences were; *Be Here Now* by Ram Dass, *Creative Visualization* by Shakti Gawain, *Emmanuel's Book* by Pat Rodegast, *Initiation* by Elizabeth Haich, and *Revelation: Birth of A New Age* by David Spangler.

Our location in the borough, "Puntas," Rincon, was the point where the Atlantic and Caribbean met, making it such a good surfing location. It was also known as a 'power point', a place where ley lines intersected and portals opened to higher realms. I was inspired to journal everyday, write poetry, make seashell jewelry and artistic crafts, meditate, and learned to do yoga with the guidance of Richard Hittlemann's Yoga book.

I loved to swim, so when there were waves, that meant swimming out behind where the waves were breaking, not to get hit by one or by a surf board. I had great respect for the ocean and realized that I was often treading in the deepest part of the Atlantic, called the Mona Trench. In retrospect, that was a brave thing to do, as there are many creatures in the sea, as well as strong currents. I prayed a lot and floated, feeling safe and protected, connected with the Sea of Love. It was exhilarating. When caught in a rift, it's best to let go and go with the flow, moving in the direction of turning of the tide.

We didn't really know what was going on in the world in the 1980's. We were in our own world, with no television, telephone, and the radio and newspapers were all in Spanish. We felt in harmony within our minds and environment, and experienced that there is no world outside of our minds. Once, we made tea from the Psilocybin mushrooms that grew in our rose garden and experienced God speaking to us through the heat lightening that was displayed for hours in the night sky over the ocean. It was enlightening!

We went back to Florida for several months in 1983 and stayed with my husband's family, after we had traveled to visit my family and friends up north. We needed to make some money, so he did construction jobs, while I got my job back at the Day Care Center. We also commercially grew alfalfa sprouts that we sold to local restaurants.

My husband's father was influential in my continuing education on the communist-socialist conspiracy to enslave America, through his connection to the John Birch Society, which was often dismissed as "lunatic fringe." Its founder Robert Welch began the society with the purpose, "to awaken a sleeping and apathetic people concerning the designs of those who are working to destroy our constitutional republic."

When looking to connect with kindred spirits in our community, I looked up churches in the local phone book. Under the listing for non-denominational churches, I found, "Unity: A Center of Light and Love," and instantly met some spiritual friends. During our time there, I worked at Unity as a Sunday School Teacher, led a weekly meditation group, and was a clerk in the metaphysical bookstore.

Returning to our home in Puerto Rico in October 1983, I had a new collection of spiritual books, and we had made sufficient money to begin construction on a new guest house. We built a two-story hexagon with a surrounding balcony and side porch. With the additional space, we could invite more visitors, which inspired us to advertise our place as, "The Open Heart Retreat." We loved sharing our island lifestyle and had many guests.

After studying many different spiritual paths, I made a conscious choice to resign as my own teacher, and I prayed to God for guidance on my path, asking for my assignment. The next day in the mail was the 3 book set of *A Course In Miracles; Text, Workbook, and Teacher's Manual*, that a friend had sent to me. It was June 1984. I recognized it as my assignment from God and it has been my path and practice ever since.

A couple of good friends in our neighborhood built a large pyramid in their backyard to use for group gatherings and various healing sessions. We worked together to co-create many celebrations over the years for equinoxes, solstices, full moons, and other events. It was around this time that we became identified as New Age cheerleaders for the new consciousness emerging, as New Age music became the new soundtrack of our movie.

We organized a big event for "The Harmonic Convergence" on August 16 and 17, 1987. The dates were an unprecedented event in which thousands of people all over the world simultaneously meditated together to usher in the New Age of love, peace, and unity. We participated in our little corner of the world with meditation, music, and celebration, feeling that we were part of the new emergence from our collective convergence.

As I was getting deeper into spiritual practices, my husband was getting deeper into pot and alcohol. We were growing apart. A series of events transpired in our personal life that led me to leave my marriage, as well as, Puerto Rico. Gathering just a few of my things, I flew to Pennsylvania to stay with my sister and family in the Spring of 1989. I was in shock with the unexpected turn of events. It was both a transition and initiation.

The Omega Institute for Holistic Studies in Rhinebeck, NY was hiring for their summer staff. My application was accepted and I soon was off to new adventures. My job in the programming department was to set up workshops and be the host for the teachers and participants. The staff was able to attend many workshops, dances, concerts, and great speakers. It was like a Metaphysical Disneyland and I was really in my element.

My friend from Puerto Rico had also joined the Omega staff. We became romantically involved. With a pending divorce, I was conflicted about being in another relationship. Although we traveled together in the fall of 1989, I still felt the need to have some time and space for myself to process all the changes. It was the turning of another decade and I, too, was turning, like the traditional Quaker song;

"Tis a gift to be simple, tis a gift to be free; Tis a gift to come down where you ought to be. And when you find yourself in the place just right, you will be in the valley of love and delight. When true simplicity is gained, to bow and to bend, we shant be ashamed; To turn, to turn, will be our delight; Till by turning, turning, we come 'round right."

Working In Spiritual Communities in the 1990's

"Life isn't measured by the breaths you take, but by the moments that take your breath away." ~Anonymous

The 1990's were a decade of adventure, change, and transition. We brought the New Year in with my family in Williamsport, PA. My sister Michele had just got divorced after 24 years of marriage and was in transition. I had helped her pack up her belongings, have a yard sale, and U haul her from her home in New Jersey to a local storage unit. Since I was in transition as well, we conspired to embark on an adventure together.

We purchased a utility van, which my artistic boyfriend transformed into a comfortable conversion van for us to live and travel in. We named it 'Pegasus', after the white winged horse, who was our protector during what became our 5 month cross-country trip, from January to May 1990. With no time schedule or other requirements, we were free to travel at our own pace. On that cold winter day, when ready to go, we headed south.

Besides the general sight-seeing, we had the specific intention of visiting some friends and spiritual communities that were described in the book, *Builders of the Dawn*. During our journey, I was reading *Spiritual Growth* by Sanaya Roman. This was the theme and purpose that provided lots of time for contemplation, journaling, letter writing, and hours of philosophical conversations, personal sharing, and reflection.

Some highlights included meeting midwife Ina May Gaskin at "The Farm" in Tennessee; the "New Age" city and great music of Austin, Texas; our past life memories at the Taos Pueblo in NM; our vortex experience in Sedona and the Grand Canyon in AZ; Attending Yogananda's Self-Realization Fellowship in LA, CA; doing one month of work exchange for lodging at Mount Madonna Center in CA; and our peak experience of Mt. Shasta, CA.

We were camping in our van on a landing up on Mt. Shasta for several days. One night, while we were just about to fall asleep, we noticed what we assumed to be bright headlights from a vehicle that pulled up behind us. We waited for the sound of someone getting out of their car, but there was silence. When we looked through the curtain on the back window, there was no car there. The light was coming from above! Intuiting that it was a UFO checking us out, I just started communicating telepathically who we were and why we were there. Then it went away.

We were on Mt. Shasta for Earth Day and were surprised to wake up to several cars coming up the mountain to where we were parked. We joined with dozens of women that gathered in a large circle to have a ceremony to bless Mother Earth, and we were amazed when it started to snow! We also participated in a local dance that evening, loving the kindred spirits that we met and the consciousness of the community.

My favorite community was, "The Emissaries of Divine Light" in Loveland, CO., who from my perspective, were demonstrating all the best qualities of a functional spiritual center. We were blessed to be at the right place at the right time to attend the 'Grand Ole Opry' in TN; New Orleans just before Mardi Grau: hear the Mormon Tabernacle Choir perform "The Messiah" on Easter Sunday, and enjoy an evening lecture with Ram Dass in MN.

When we returned to PA. in May '90. Michele moved into an apartment, and I joined the Omega Institute staff for another summer. My work this time was in the bookstore and gift shop, where I was grateful to meet all the participants that would come through, as well as, see all the latest books. My role in a "Star Trek" play at the end of the summer was memorable as Captain Kirk's girlfriend, when people fell off chairs with laughter.

The Foundation for *A Course In Miracles* was located in Roscoe, NY, just a couple of hours from Omega. My application to join the staff there was accepted, so in Sept. of 1990, I relocated into an apartment, with a beautiful view of Tennanah Lake. I was ready to settle down and study The Course that I loved, grateful to be part of the community there, and privileged to study with the respected teachers, Ken and Gloria Wapnick.

My work on staff was general care of the retreat property, which included preparation of meals during conferences, and housekeeping of the guest rooms, lodge, and offices. My spiritual work was application of the Course principles, which was much deeper and more difficult than I had expected. With the opportunity to attend Ken's classes, I soon realized that there was much more to learn and experience.

It was the best of times with the honor of this personal mentorship, and the worst of times with the ego undoing we all experienced and the forgiveness lessons presented. My 33 year old ego complained that this wasn't fun, it was too cold most of the year, there were strained relationships with the staff, and I was bored, isolated, and restless. After two years of life changing time there, I was ready for my next adventure.

In Sept. 1992, I joined the staff of Edgar Cayce's Association for Research and Enlightenment and relocated to Virginia Beach. Having met a man that worked there who was attending a Course conference, I was invited to visit, and applied for a job. Located on the beach, the A.R.E. was a fun place to be, with much warmer weather, an active community, and the second largest metaphysical library in the world.

My first year there, I worked in the bookstore and gift shop at the Visitor's Center. It was an ideal place to meet people, review the new books, attend conferences, and play lots of new age music, which was the soundtrack of the time. My apartment was next to the A.R.E. and across from the beach, so I was in my element again. As *A Course In Miracles* teacher, I soon gave a workshop for a group of students, and continued with weekly Course groups during the five years I was there.

The next year I was hired as the Correspondence Coordinator in the Membership Dept. My job was to answer all the letters that came into the A.R.E., answer the 800 hotline for requests about the Cayce readings, health remedies, dream interpretation, and help for disturbing psychic and paranormal experiences. My spiritual counseling and writing skills were activated, and I felt aligned with my higher purpose.

After receiving instruction on public speaking, I became a weekly survey lecturer at the Visitor's Center, where I gave many talks on the Cayce readings. One class I wrote was on the "Spirit of Service" and another was "Mind, Soul, and Spirit." Charles Thomas Cayce asked me to facilitate groups during the annual "Finding Your Mission In Life" conference and the "Cooperative Family; Parent/Child" conference.

Many happy memories of friendships made there and much enjoyment from working with the staff. It was meaningful to be able to attend all the conferences for free, too. One highlight was the conference when Ken and Gloria Wapnick came to lecture about *A Course In Miracles*, and I was privileged to give a little talk of introduction to Ken. My heart is truly dedicated to the Course and Ken will always be my friend and teacher.

It was at an A.R.E. conference, appropriately called, "Gateway To The Future," that I met my future husband. He was from Wichita, KS., so we had a long distance relationship of long phone calls. We flew back and forth to visit each other, and then he proposed to me. Since we had both been married before, we had a small wedding at the A.R.E. meditation garden in May, 1997, and we were off on another adventure.

Packing my belongings into a U Haul trailer, we headed west into the sunset, and to my new home in Kansas, where he lived with his two sons, ages 10 and 13, and a golden retriever puppy. My new family also included his parents, two brothers, and other relatives. My heart was opened and expanded with my new loving relationships and my new life in general, in the 'heart'land, with lots of jokes about Dorothy and *The Wizard of Oz*.

My husband was self-employed as an owner of business properties, which allowed him to work from home and allowed us free time to travel. In addition to road trips to visit his brother in Colorado, we drove to southern Texas to visit my friend, and went over the border into Mexico. We made road trips to Pennsylvania to visit my family, too, and took my sisters into Arkansas when they visited our home in Wichita.

The big trip that we took together was to Egypt. It was a two week A.R.E. Tour in 1999, where I was asked to host the small group of tourists as a representative of A.R.E., since the regular tour guide was unable to go. Fortunately we had a respected Egyptian tour guide to lead our group, so I was just an assistant to help with facilitation. It was a 22 hour flight where we met him at the airport in Cairo.

Our tour guide was a fifth generation archaeologist who lived on Sphinx St. in the heart of the Giza Plateau. He took us to his home for a roof top view of the Sphinx and the pyramids, where we enjoyed the sunset over the Sahara. His wife made us a home cooked meal of the local specialties, as we discussed the plans for the tour, before taking us to our elegant rooms at the five star Cairo Hotel.

Our first day included a close up and personal experience with the Sphinx, as we shared Edgar Cayce's readings about the Hall of Records located under its front right paw. We were giddy during our camel ride around the Giza Plateau at sunset. We studied the three main pyramids of Giza, and were so fortunate to be given the opportunity to spend two hours inside The Great Pyramid that evening, alone, with our little tour group of ten.

Certainly a highlight of the trip, and up there with the most memorable experiences of my life, was the journey into The Great Pyramid of Giza. The descending chamber was a narrow passage down that was too claustrophobic for me to attempt, but we easily went up into the well-lit ascending tunnels. We tuned into the amazing acoustics as we chanted Om together in the Queen's Chamber and took turns laying in the open granite sarcophagus in the King's Chamber, where Jesus was said to have had an initiation. The enormous granite blocks on the inside fit together with such great precision, that it was clearly made with unknown technologies, and I joked that the blocks 'seamed' perfect.

We were thrilled with the collection of artifacts and exhibits at the Cairo Museum, along with tours of the oldest church in Egypt, and the Citidal and Mosque of Mohammed Ali. Each day was an exploration of another sacred temple site. We flew to Luxor to embark on our Nile Cruise ship, stopping along the way to see more enormous and magnificent temples, where ancient history was illustrated and written in stone. We managed to stay healthy and avoided the dreaded amoeba poisoning, while enjoying the delicious foods, and only drinking bottled water. The Egyptian experience was complete with belly dancers and whirling dervishes as entertainment, and some souvenirs and gifts.

We attended a Sedona conference in early 1999 with the theme of disclosure of 'Earth Mysteries' with cutting-edge information from current authors like astronaut Edgar Mitchell, mind-control survivor Brice Taylor, conspiracy investigator, Jim Marrs, UFO investigator Linda Moulton Howe, futurist, Chet Snow, archaeologist Zacharia Setchin, astrologer Julie Gillentine, Pleiadian channeler, Barbara Marciniak, and David Icke.

Back home, our life was basically quiet with a smooth jazz soundtrack. We attended all the boys sporting events at school and took our dog for daily walks. My husband's hobby was water skiing, and it is hard to imagine that he had me actually doing stunts like standing on the skier's shoulders to form a pyramid! I learned to water ski, and loved to swim in the lake. We both loved to read and explore bookstores.

The disclosure bestsellers of the 1990's were David Icke, *And The Truth Shall Set You Free*, and other tapes and videos; Bob Frissell's, *Nothing In This Book Is True, But It's Exactly How Things Are*; and G.Edward Griffin's, *The Creature From Jekyll Island: a second look at the Federal Reserve*. We all were tuning into, Coast to Coast AM Radio with Art Bell, who kept us up on the real "rest of the story," not the Paul Harvey version.

Cathy O'Brien's book, *Trance Formation of America*, written in 1995, tells her story of surviving decades of the CIA's MKUltra Project Monarch mind control operation. She was groomed as a sex slave, as part of human and drug trafficking programs. Her first hand experiences communicated the insidious situations as a whistleblower. Yet her courage to escape and be deprogrammed offers hope for empowerment and healing.

We were all waiting on the earth changes, the pole shift, and Edgar Cayce's and Gordon Michael Scallion's predictions of the new map of America after these events. Then there was the dreaded Y2K at the turn of the New Millennium, when the computers could go down, along with the internet, and the grid systems. We were stocking up on our emergency foods and supplies, as practical preppers for the coming changes.

In 1999, *The Matrix*, one of the most important films of our generation was released. If you can look beyond the violence and futuristic sci-fi, you can receive the messages that are revealed, as shown here with some important quotes from the movie;

Trinity: "You know the question just as I did."

Neo: "What is the matrix?"

Trinity: "The answer is out there, Neo. It is looking for you. And it will find you if you want it to."

Morpheus: "You take the blue pill, the story ends, you wake up in your bed and believe whatever you want to believe. You take the red pill, you stay in wonderland, and I show you how deep the rabbit hole goes."

Morpheus: "The Matrix is everywhere, it is all around us, even now in this very room. You can see it when you look outside your window, or turn on your television. You can feel it when you go to work, when you go to church, when you pay your taxes. It is the world that has been pulled over your eyes to blind you from the truth."

Neo: "What truth?"

Morpheus: "That you are a slave Neo. Like everyone else, you were born into bondage...born into a prison that you cannot smell or taste or touch. A prison for your mind. You have to let it all go, Neo...fear, doubt, and disbelief. Free Your Mind."

Morpheus: "I'm trying to free your mind, Neo. But I can only show you the door. You're the one that has to walk through it."

Morpheus: (holding a battery) "The Matrix is a computer-generated dreamworld built to keep us under control in order to change the human being into one of these."

Morpheus: "You have to understand, most of these people are not ready to be unplugged. And many of them are so inured, so hopelessly dependent on the system, that they will fight to protect it."

Young Monk: "Do not try to bend the spoon...that is impossible. Instead only try to realize the truth."

Neo: "What truth?"

Young Monk: "There is no spoon."

Prince told us all to "party like it's 1999." The fireworks were exceptional on that New Year's Eve as we all turned the calendar into the 21st Century. Louise Hay summed it up best in her little book *Millennium 2000; A Positive Approach*;

"Remember Dear Friends, We have the opportunity to step out of the victim role, and by changing the way we think, become master's of our life. The millennium awaits those who are ready to advance themselves spiritually. If we are willing to release the emotional attachments to beliefs and limitations from the past, then we can live fully in the new moment."

Holistic Health Educators In The 2000's

"There are only two ways to live your life. One is as though nothing is a miracle. The other is as though everything is a miracle." ~Albert Einstein

Our timeline turned into the New Millennium, the Y2K was a non-event, and yet we all were feeling the changes that were looming, both personally and collectively. Interesting to see how the beginning of each new decade marked a major turning point in my life. The issue at the time was with my marriage, as a series of events led me to the realization of being in an unhealthy relationship that would escalate into a divorce.

In retrospect, it was both traumatic and transformative, in that the challenges we had to endure were also profound growth opportunities. If all is well that ends well, we can agree that the lessons learned were worth the damage done. In the midst of going through the process of asking for help, I received so much guidance, including a book falling off the shelf to teach me about, *The Verbally Abusive Relationship*.

Our personal relationships are such good classrooms. Understanding the ego's projections from ones inner, suppressed pain, allows us to not take things personally. Learning that you can love someone without them being right for you. Learning what you can change and want you cannot. To agree to disagree without resentment or blame, to be able to lovingly accept, forgive, and have a peaceful closure, was a miracle.

By the Spring of 2000, we were not in Kansas anymore. Life had propelled me in new directions. Like our cross-country adventure in 1990, my sister now was helping me drive my car and U-Haul truck east to Williamsport, PA to begin a new chapter in my life. Moving into my own apartment, working to reach a divorce settlement, and applying for a new job at the local health food store, appropriately called, 'Freshlife'.

The store owner hired me and became an expert mentor in my new position as a Vitamin Consultant and Wellness Coach. Holistic Health was one of my passions, so the work was an ideal situation, both as a student and a teacher, it was fertile ground for the next 7 years. Grateful to be living in the same town as my family, making new friendships, and feeling connected to the local community.

On September 11, 2001, our world was changed by a terrorist attack. The television played images of a plane flying into the Twin Towers in NYC, that later dissolved into rubble and clouds of smoke. Scenes of traumatized people running, some leaping to their death from the building, and horror and panic everywhere. Reports of those that were missing and presumed dead. We watched in shock as the tragedy unfolded.

It was the dawning of the age of terrorism. We were on red alert for potential attacks and suspicious about who the terrorists were. George Bush was quick to implement the Patriot Act to protect us from these evil doers, while taking away an increasing number of our freedoms. The fact that our nation was grieving such a massive loss of life made us more willing to give our power away to searches and scanners, all to keep us safe.

When building 7 free fell like a bombing demolition, suspicions were raised in question of the official narrative. A series of documentaries revealed factual information, including evidence from the coalition of architects and engineers in, *9/11 - Explosive Evidence - Experts Speak Out, 9/11 Conspiracy Theories and The Unanswered Questions, Zeitgeist, Loose Change 9/11*, and Michael Moore's *Fahrenheit 9/11*.

The implications of the 9/11 event being an inside job made this the mother of all conspiracies. The more we would look at the inconsistencies, the bending of the laws of physics, the absurd political 'facts', and the cover-ups of crimes, the more we would question. The best synopsis was in Judy Wood's book, *Where Did The Towers Go? - Evidence of Directed Free-Energy Technology on 9/11.*

In 2002, Aaron Russo, director of the documentary, *America: Freedom or Fascism*, shared an interview he had with David Rockefeller. When asked what was the ultimate purpose of 'the New World Order agenda', he revealed the One World Government plans to reduce the population and control the rest through microchip implants. Could this be the disclosure of a psychopathic agenda to commit crimes against humanity?

David Icke had written extensively about these psychopaths that comprised about 1% of our population, at the top of the pyramid of control. Known as the IIluminati, the Cabal, the Deep State, and the Committee of 300, that includes the Elite Bloodlines, Jesuits, Freemasons, Secret Societies, The United Nations, Club of Rome, The Bilderberg Group, Council on Foreign Relations, Zionists, Satanists, and Pedophiles.

We have reached the part in our story where the Hero meets the Nemesis. It is the difficult part, the part we rather not see or talk about. It feels uncomfortable, fear producing, and difficult to take in. Our response is to reject it, deny it, and go into a state of 'cognitive dissonance'. One of the greatest tricks of the devil is to pretend he does not exist. Evil has to present itself as good.

Bringing to light all that has been hidden from us gets to the cause of the problem. Once we can see the puppet masters that have been pulling the strings behind the scenes, we can be empowered to cut the cords that have been manipulating us. By not looking, we are giving our consent to allow them to continue with their nefarious agenda. We can become change agents by opening our minds to change.

Throughout my "one loving life," this information has been consistently coming to me, and I consider it my 'assignment' to look at it with the Holy Spirit, that is, to look at it without judgment. As the new psychics has taught us, we change the quantum field by our observation of it. Accepting the role of a conspiracy observer, blows the cover off the deception and we can stand in the Truth of Our Being, The Eternal Love That We Are.

I credit David Icke with his deep dive into the disclosure of the few who would enslave the many, by persevering through derogatory labels and dismissals as a lunatic. Two quotes of his specifically define our task at this time;

> "Stop acquiescing and participating in your own enslavement in any area of your life." and "If you are fighting the system, you are still caught in it. The ultimate revolution is expressing Who You Really Are." ~David Icke

I credit *A Course In Miracles* that teaches that there is no world outside of our minds. It is only our minds that need to change, by identifying with our One Loving Self, united with our Creator, not our separated, fearful egos. Its metaphysics helps us to stay above the battleground of dueling duality, allowing miracles to replace murder, by choosing forgiveness of illusions, and remembering our shared identity as God Created Us.

> "Spirit am I, a holy Son of God, free of all limits, safe and healed and whole, free to forgive, and free to save the world." ~A Course In Miracles Wk Lesson 97; 7; 2

It was in 2003, when I was feeling whole within myself and in true relationship with God, that my life partner showed up. David was hired as the manager of 'Freshlife' and we both felt the comfortability and ease of being in the presence of soul family. We are truly on the same wave length and it felt good just to know that we were together in the same movie. Work became more meaningful and enjoyable.

Our talks in the vitamin aisle became more frequent and deeper, until one day, at the end of our work shift at 5:00, we decided to continue our conversation over dinner. After talking incessantly for hours, we were so surprised that we were closing the restaurant down at 10:30. It was then that we realized our undeniable connection, but we both agreed that we were not available to date, because of the manager/ employee situation.

We started talking on the phone after work in the evenings. Away from the potentially judgmental eyes of others, we were free to pursue our friendship. I started to see a counselor for guidance, and it was in one of those sessions that I realized my love for David. When sharing my epiphany with him on the phone that night, he came directly over to my apartment to give me a memorable kiss, to let me know it was mutual.

The staff all laughed at us when we told them we were in love, because even though we thought we were hiding it, they all knew. David moved into my apartment in August 2003, we got engaged in February, and were married in July 2004. We had a beautiful wedding in a gazebo at my sister Karen and brother-in-law Jack's property with just our immediate family, and danced into the summer night, celebrating our one loving life together.

In the fall of 2004, we went to a conference at the A.R.E. In Virginia Beach to see our beloved teachers Ken and Gloria Wapnick. They took us out to dinner as a wedding gift, and gave us their blessing for a long, happy marriage. It was during a long beach walk at that time, that I had the vision of buying a house in Williamsport. We contacted a realtor, and as soon as we returned, found our house on the second day of looking.

We closed on our home in November 2005 and are still living in it at the time of this writing. Located less than a mile from our apartment, it was an easy move, and a joy to decorate our beautiful, 4 story, 4 bedroom home, with 4 tall, old Norway Spruce trees in our fenced in backyard. Built in the 1920's, where a family named "Love" raised their family and lived for many decades. We called it the house that Love built.

Our home became the sacred space for many gatherings of friends and family. Our large dining table would be the scene of groups for celebrations and holiday dinners. Our living room would accommodate meditation, healing, and discussion groups, Course In Miracles groups, and ceremonies for Solstices, Equinoxes, Full Moons, and astrological dates of significance. We had a spiritual community of friends.

One night before our group came, we saw a crow with a broken wing hopping around our yard. We fed it during the week it was there. David communed with it and sent it healing energy from his hands. Then it flew away. A week later, just before our group was due to come again, David saw the same crow on an electrical wire. They made eye contact and felt so much gratitude empathically communicated, that it made him cry.

Our work at "Freshlife" was increasingly successful as a booming health food store, where we educated people in natural ways to take responsibility for their own health. It was a demanding workday of counseling customers, training staff, ordering products, decorating the store, making displays, posters, and writing a weekly column for an electronic newsletter. We were most grateful for all the people that we could help.

The next turning point was when I intuitively felt that my work at Freshlife was complete and something new was coming. It was in July of 2007, after training my replacement and resigning, that my new assignment emerged. After writing 'morning pages' everyday, I soon discovered that a book was being created. It was called, *The Heart of The Matter*, about our multi-dimensional heart and becoming wholehearted.

Feeling inspired and joyfully motivated, the creative process kept me on task until it was completed. Illustrated with collages that I crafted to represent all the individual pieces that come together to form a whole 'peace' of art, it felt like a thesis of my spiritual journey and path with heart. David helped me with the type setting and editing, so that we could self publish it together in early 2008.

We planned a book signing tour in conjunction with a trip to the southwest to attend a Drunvalo Melchizedek workshop in Sedona and Course In Miracles workshop in CA. in the spring of 2008. It was exciting to receive our published book copies and had some mailed ahead to our destinations. Renting a car, we drove to visit friends in Taos, NM., where we had a book signing and gave a lecture at the Noetic Sciences Community.

Returning home to Williamsport, we promoted the book locally with lectures and book signings at First Friday events, stores, and art shows. The original collages were on display in a local gallery where I was the featured artist of the month and presented a personal poetry reading one evening. *The Heart of the Matter* also became an ebook and a fun creative process that I really put my heart into.

Our next creative project was hosting my own radio show, "Good Vibrations for your Body, Mind, and Spirit," a one hour, weekly program providing educational and inspirational information about holistic health. We also had clients for personal and holistic health consultations, as we formed our own business called "HealThySelf."

David had left 'Freshlife' as well, so we became self-employed with our health products and services, while working from home. We had several creative projects, including regular Native American sweat lodges that we would organize with friends. Our sacred circles and ceremonies were a big part of our spiritual life. Our group all contributed to buying an agricultural healing tool called a "Harmonizer." When activated with sound, such as a CD, the environmental protection was extended to a 60 mile radius. We have continued to consistently play healing sound CD's into the Harmonizer in our home since 2009, and are amazed by its various beneficial effects.

The worldly mischief of 2008-2009 was the financial collapse and bail out of banks. Wall St. and the banking cartels were the cause of this financial crisis, by using mortgage backed securities as fraudulent collateral. The disclosure of this crime exposed that the real Coup D-Etat in the United States was financial not military. The book, *The Big Short; Inside the Doomsday Machine*, later became a disclosure film.

G. Edward Griffin educated us about the money mafia and the men who met in secret to create the Federal Reserve at Jekyll Island. He explains that it is not federal and there are no reserves. President Kennedy was planning to take down the Federal Reserve and take our US dollar from fiat to gold backed currency. The people's power was usurped by the private criminal syndicate banking system, by lending money that doesn't exist and charging interest on it. This contributed to our economic slavery.

Our soundtrack for the 2000's was, "The Blues." Not in a sad way, but a truly joyful way. David and I loved to go to the local Blues Festival every year and dance all day. We just loved the beat, the notes, and the way the music made us feel and want to move. It was truly a form of ecstatic dancing for us, lifting our frequency while we were celebrating life through the frequency of The Blues.

Practical Mystics in the 2010's

"Life is pure adventure and the sooner we realize that, the quicker we will be able to treat life as art." ~Maya Angelou

2010 was another turning point year to initiate the new decade. In the first half of the year, our creative projects included giving various lectures and workshops. We are both teachers and students, as we teach what we want to learn. Interestingly, we began the year talking about some transformational concepts and in the second half, we really got to apply them. After all, the best way to teach is to demonstrate.

In January, David and I were asked to talk at a local church, and we titled our lecture, "The Shift In Consciousness; Practical Living In The New Paradigm." In March, my lecture to the Chamber of Commerce was, "The New Paradigm of Business; A Shift from Competition to Cooperation." Both talks were well-received by the groups, and it made me realize how inspiring others inspired us.

In March and April, David and I gave two different three day workshops that were more experiential and we could go deeper. One was "The Spring Equinox Awakening The Heart" and the other was, "Remembering Who We Are; Integrating Science and Spirit for a Relevant Approach To Our Times." It felt so good to be able to share what we were realizing and experiencing at the time with interactive groups.

In May, we were invited to give a talk at the Science and Spirituality Meditation Center in Bowling Green, VA., as part of their "Transformation To Oneness Conference." My topic was, "Becoming One With Ourselves: The Shift From Separation To Wholeness." Since it was a weekend workshop at a retreat center, we were joined by a couple of car loads of friends from Williamsport who went with us.

It was there that we met Audri Scott Williams, another speaker at the conference, and also someone that we both recognized as soul family. Audri identified herself as a world peace walker, author, mystic, mother, and grandmother, proud of her heritage as part African, Cherokee, and Irish. We had an instant connection, and along with our local friends, we invited her to come to Williamsport to facilitate a workshop with us.

In June, Audri arrived in Williamsport to celebrate her 55th birthday, along with her partner, Karen Hunter Watson. We organized speaking engagements for her at the YWCA and The Center, and the occasion of her arrival made the headlines on the front page of the Sun-Gazette; "Human Rights Activist To Speak." My sister hosted a 5 day retreat workshop at her home for Audri, Karen, and our group of friends.

Audri and Karen shared their plans for a peace walk across America that was called, "13 Moon Walk 4 Peace," from 10-10-10 to 11-11-11. The purpose of the 13 month journey was "to awaken the heart of America, bringing visibility to the invisible and voice to the voiceless; to affect healing and transform the way we relate to one another." We had agreed to help her in some way, and had no idea at the time how much!

In following our hearts, our intuition knows the right thing to do before the head has it all figured out. Our decision to be part of the 13 Moon Walk 4 Peace gradually dawned on us, like an idea whose time had come, it felt like a calling. Then there is the philosophy that we don't so much have regrets in life for what we have done, but for what we didn't do and wish we had.

When Audri offered us the opportunity to be national coordinators, we were honored and grateful for the chance to be of service in such a meaningful way. We respected Audri as a wise teacher and leader and felt privileged to work with her. It felt like the time to "walk our talk" for inner peace and "be the change you want to see in the world." To demonstrate this message was to strengthen the idea and manifest positive change.

In August, David and I took a trip with my sister Karen and brother-in-law Jack to visit our cousin in Nova Scotia. We drove north to Portland, Maine and took a scenic ferry ride into Canada. In addition to being a fun vacation, it was an opportunity to facilitate another workshop called, "The Heart of Healing; A Gathering of Kindred Spirits." All of these workshops seemed to be preparing us for what was to come.

In September, we drove with some local friends to the Peace Bridge in Buffalo, NY to receive a sacred flame for the peace walk, that was ceremoniously passed onto us to fulfill a prophecy from the Iroquois Six Nations in Canada. The peace walkers were honored to carry the Eternal Flame of Spiritual Democracy known as the Sacred Flame of the Thunder, symbolizing the Iroquois Great Law of Peace. Returning to Williamsport where the peace team organized a community walk with the sacred flame, then driving it for a ceremony at our Nation's Capitol, where we passed it onto Audri and Karen.

The Sacred Flame of the Thunder was to be united with the Eternal Flame at the King Center in Atlanta, GA to launch the official beginning of the 13 Moon Walk 4 Peace on October 10. On the same date, the 13 Indigenous Grandmothers were gathering to present a workshop at the Omega Institute in NY. Our intuitive friend was so certain that David and I should meet with them that she bought us tickets. It was meant to be.

We went with a small group to spend a week with these extraordinary wisdom keepers. Our first evening at Omega, we met two women planning to attend the conference, but had no place to stay, so we invited them to share our large room. We were surprised that each had a sacred crystal skull with them and wonder if we were downloaded in some way while sleeping each night with the skulls next to our bed.

One of the skulls belonged to Grandmother Flordemayo, who David knew from attending a ceremony at her home in New Mexico years ago. During the conference, we were able to ask a question of the Grandmothers. In telling them about our plans for the peace walk and asking for their blessing, we were delighted when Flordemayo came down from the stage to hug David, saying she was glad to see he was continuing his work.

The Grandmothers did bless us in many ways. We were given permission to show their documentary, *For The Next 7 Generations* in several cities around the country. We met up with several of the Grandmothers during an event when we were in Berkley, CA. Two of the Grandmothers invited us to their home at the Pine Ridge Reservation, SD., where we were honored to participate in a sweat lodge with them, meet with their son, the 7th generation of Sitting Bull, and plant a customized peace pole on the reservation.

On our drive home from Omega, we saw a 24 ft. motor home with a "for sale" sign on the side of the road. When stopping to look inside, we saw a wooden sign, "home sweet home" and took it as a sign that this might be our home during the 13 month journey. We knew it was meant to be, when the price that the owner wanted was the same amount that our friend Dick gave us as a gift donation towards the walk. We drove back to buy it the next day. With "HG" on the license plate, we named her "Harmony Grace."

When we made the commitment to go, everything came together. Jim offered to stay in our house and pay our mortgage while we were gone. Sandi offered to help with the housekeeping, plants, mail, and other expenses that came up. Melodie gave us peace scarves and Angela made beaded peace bracelets to sell to make money. Alice held a yard sale to raise money for the walk. We were supported and all our needs were met.

We left on the October full moon, heading south in our packed RV, "Harmony Grace." Audri had warned us that these journeys tend to bring up all of our fears, and indeed, my list of "what ifs" all happened. When we arrived in Valdosta, GA two days later to join with the peace walk, our adventure of a lifetime really began. Nothing was like we thought it would be and we were stressed and stretched way out of our comfort zones.

It was truly a mystical journey full of initiations. Audri was the Vision Keeper of the Walk, who was guided by four Grandmothers in Spirit. Some helpful words of guidance were; "What was important yesterday is not important today. Just follow the energy. Things change. Go with the flow. Keep working it." There was also another realistic expression she would often say, "Everything will be as clear as mud."

My multi-tasking skills were put to good use in outreaching to each community on our route to speak in various churches, schools, government agencies, radio stations, and community centers. Coordinating service projects, local 'walk-a-mile-for-peace' groups, peace pole production, film screenings, and press releases. We recorded 100's of videos asking people what peace meant to them, while we demonstrated our PEACE acronym; Passionately Engaged Affecting Community Everywhere.

We would walk multiple miles almost everyday. We would map out a proposed distance and each walker would cover a portion of the mileage. One person would park the car before their walk, and the one who walked to the car would pick everyone else up. We had a scenic tour of the country, from the busy downtown streets to the middle of nowhere, we saw the wealthiest and poorest neighborhoods, and many kindred spirits.

The 13 Moon Walk for Peace planted 40 customized peace poles around the country. Each community would choose three meaningful words, in addition to PEACE, and on a 4x4x8 wooden post, we would draw, carve, wood burn, and paint each letter, along with our turtle logo. These 'towers of power' with a crystal wrapped in copper inside and bronze plaque on the outside, united our communities together in peace.

Some memorable public highlights include receiving the Hero's Award for the Season of Non-Violence from at the Agape Spiritual Center in LA., CA.; presenting a televised conference on Conflict Resolution at the Monterey Institute of International Studies; being invited to join traditional ceremonies with Native American tribes in Yuma, AZ, Pine Ridge, SD, Oneida, WI, Lansing, MI, Franklin, NC; and our closing awards ceremony in Atlanta, GA, on 11-11-11, honoring the unsung heroes we met along the way.

There were many memorable personal highlights, so many that we could write a book on just this life changing experience. With several notebooks full of daily journal entries, our schedule of events in each community, we have lots of stories to tell. We often said that everyday felt like a week, each week felt like a month, and instead of being gone for 13 months, it felt like 13 years! Time was so surreal and timeless at the same time.

One of the ironies was all the time we spent trying to get sponsors, to no avail. Our only sponsors were our community of friends and family from Williamsport. Karen and Jack actually drove our Honda Element from home to meet us in Phoenix, through cold winter snow storms in February. They put new tires on our car, and arrived with several care packages of food and gifts, cards, and money from our group. They also flew to Atlanta, along with a few friends, to attend our closing ceremony and then drove home with us.

Our favorite, mystical story of the trip was in Austin, TX., during our water healing ceremony at Barton Springs; a beautiful pool with a vortex of freshwater welling up. We made our altar and gathered a circle of locals to celebrate with us. Audri had us walk around the pool sending our prayers to the water. We sang our water healing songs and soon musicians started to jam, we all began dancing, and the energy was high.

David was in a whirling dervish reverie and soon discovered that he had lost his glasses and his wedding ring. We went back several times hoping to find it, but the water was murky with plants. A couple of nights later, after lots of prayers for help, David had a dream that he was swimming in the springs with the Lady of the Lake, whom he asked to help him find the ring.

The next day, after David went with Audri and Karen for an acupuncture treatment, they drove to an empty lot where there once was a crystal shop. When David was returning into the car, he saw Audri in the backseat with her hand out and a strange look on her face. She felt his ring coming from another dimension and almost caught it, as it landed on the floor by David's feet! It was our mystical, "Return of the Ring!" It was a miracle!

This was one of so many blessings that we received during the peace walk. I actually made a staggering long list of all the intentional prayers, blessing ceremonies, initiations, labyrinth walks, sacred items gifted, sacred peace pipe ceremonies, sacred sites, sacred messages, agnihotra ceremonies, blessing of The Dao, The Great Peace Flame of the Thunder, transmissions from Indigenous Elders, Monks, Ministers, Nuns, and all the generous gifts of grace. The whole experience was a Divine Orchestration.

We arrived home on November 15, 2011, to a clean house and dinner made by friends, including a welcome home circle of 14 friends that night in our living room. We felt so loved and grateful for all the support. It was great to be home and back in our own bed. We woke up during the night wondering where we were. Was it all a dream?

Our local community had celebrated our peace walk with awards and wanted a couple more customized peace poles planted. We were also asked to lead a peace walk in commemoration of MLK, Jr. Day in January, which has since become an annual event. A local community center, Firetree Place, asked me to create an art display of posters with photographs and memorabilia called "Piece Together Peace" illustrating our walk.

In Feb. 2012, we hosted a screening of the unconventional documentary, *Thrive* at our Community Arts Center, which lifts the veil on what is really going on in our world of global domination and offering real solutions to reclaim our lives and our future. We also sold copies of David Wilcock's book, *The Source Field Investigations* to awaken people to the breakthroughs in science, consciousness, time, space, and disclosure.

David's 75 year old Mother decided to sell her family home and move into The Williamsport Home. In the spring and summer of 2012, we helped her sort through and organize generations of possessions and prepare for yard sales and an auction. She easily sold her house in August, then we helped her buy new furnishings and move into her new little apartment. She was happy to make the right move at the right time.

Our family was a central part of our life. We lived within a mile from David's Mom and my four siblings. Keeping in touch with routine calls and get-togethers, including dinner parties for all the holidays and birthday celebrations, we were grateful to all be so close. In addition to hosting family gatherings, I enjoyed making games for us to play, which created some of our favorite memories...laughing together as we celebrated life.

While we were reactivating our HealThySelf consulting business and product sales, I presented Course In Miracles workshops in upstate NY, in the spring and fall of 2012. It took us awhile to reorient and reintegrate into making a regular income again. After updating my resume, I creatively looked to design new work and to find my niche. Our goal was to be practical mystics, both grounded on earth and aligned with the Divine.

The predictions of a cosmic event and collective consciousness shift occurring on the winter solstice of 2012 did not happen as we expected. Perhaps we were waiting for the world to change instead of changing our minds about the world. Perhaps we have the power to awaken from the illusion of the world by Identifying with Love, The Peace of God, and the Truth that sets us free, here and now. We realized that we were frequency holders, instruments of that Love, Peace, and Truth living in the present moment, and life was our spiritual practice. We trusted the Divine Plan.

In reviewing my daily journals throughout the years, a common theme was always in seeking our true work in alignment with our higher purpose. It has been a lifelong process of identifying what we "do." Often the realization would come that we have been fulfilling our purpose all the time, by simply "being" who we are. Yet we also wanted to be financially successful, and this is the part that often eluded us.

We had all the typical blocks to money that hold spiritual people back, like it is not right to receive money for our services because it should be self-less and free. The beliefs that no one becomes a healer to make money anyway and that marketing feels like a hustle. It has been a continual process of learning the value of what we have to offer and how to transform our beliefs to attract abundance on all levels.

In 2013, a friend delivered a prototype of a Tesla coil device to David, in the hope that he would be able to produce some empirical evidence as to how it worked. We began doing weekly tests and assessments with a small group of friends and sharing it with the inventor. David's scientific expertise and excellent customer service earned him the respect of the Biocharger company that gave him a full time position, with research and development of frequency recipes, education, documentation, and customer support.

My work projects were diverse and creative, though not consistently lucrative. In 2014, I became a non-denominational minister and wedding officiant, ordained by the Universal Life Church Monastery. Performing several local marriage ceremonies, which included counseling the couples, writing the ceremony, orchestrating the rehearsal and wedding, and obtaining the legal marriage license. It was a meaningful celebration of love.

My next original business idea was called, "Divine Order" began in 2015. Creating the service of a personal organizer, helping people get their houses and work spaces in order; decluttering, rearranging, packing, providing yard sales, help with moving, and set up. Creating the feeling that everything is in Divine Order was a good way to express my organizational skills and helpful to several appreciative clients.

In 2016 -2017, we created a blog on *The Heart of the Matter* website called "It's About Time; The Energy of the Day Report." Based on a combination of Mayan calendar solar signs and numbers 20 and 13, astrology, and numerology information of the day, we would write inspirational messages, along with wisdom from prophecies about these evolutionary cycles of time. We posted everyday for a year and a half.

The Beloved Community Council was a volunteer project from 2011-2019, where David and I served on the Board of this MLK, Jr committee. We co-created the mission statement, planned events for the annual Dream Week activities, and participated in service projects, round table discussions, and the annual community peace walk. As the Program Director, my work engaged a multi-cultural awareness in our community.

The Heart of Williamsport community outreach and networking project began in 2016. My work as the Assistant Project Coordinator involved facilitating many public events, focus groups, round table discussions, and meetings to work with volunteers. With the purpose of identifying what people value to develop vision statements to guide in local decision-making, it was very interactive with the whole community for four years.

In the spring of 2018, Akasha Center for Holistic Medicine was a new business in the old Freshlife building. Although it didn't make it financially and closed within its first year, it was fun while it lasted. The owner hired me to create a retail store, which I got to design, order inventory, set up, stock, decorate, and open in short time. Writing press releases, articles, emails, flyers, and invitations for the Grand Opening; planning and presenting group classes and educational programs, too.

In the fall of 2018, David and I rented a large 1100 sq.ft. studio as an office space among a large community of artists and businesses, called The Pajama Factory. We called our studio, "WholeheARTed Wholistic; Life Is Your 'Peace' Of Art." We decorated our beautiful space where we sold our nutritional products, held sessions with the Biocharger, facilitated groups and workshops, and David produced Schweitzer Formula.

David has been manufacturing a solution called Schweitzer Formula since 2008. This product has not only been a consistent source of income all of these years, but it has helped so many people in many ways. He built the website, developed educational material, produced, packaged, and shipped it all over the world. We have worked together on writing, education, promotion, and presentations at health fairs.

In our personal community of friends, we conducted the sacred ceremony of the Native American sweat lodges for seven years. I was part of a women's "Journey Group" for three years, and took a weekly homemade dinner to the home of our friend and Spiritual Elder for seven years. We hosted regular meditation and discussion groups, and bimonthly Course in Miracles workshops in our living room since 2006. Life was full.

The sound track of the decade was a combination of Smooth Jazz, New Age Music, including Deva Premal, Tom Kenyon chants, and Shamanic drumming. We continued to dance at the annual blues festival events. We were moving away from playing CD's and began going online with Pandora, Radio Paradise, or making playlists on our cellphones to play through our Bose speaker.

In September 2019, we embarked on another mystical adventure to visit our friend in New Mexico and Colorado. In Taos, we went to a Sting concert in a park, The Hanuman Temple, The Pueblo, and hiked to a secluded, natural hot springs in the Rio Grande. In Crestone, we stayed at I Am Harmony guesthouse, full of sacred site activations, where we visited Ashrams and other Spiritual Centers, blessed with sacred ceremonies.

The decade ended with the best gift when we brought home our Golden Retriever puppy in October 2019. We appropriately named him "Magi, All Loving and Wise," because he has been one of the best things that ever happened to us; full of unconditional love, joy, and just pure goodness. In the true spirit of the rebirth of Christ Consciousness within humanity, we have most gratefully received the gifts of the Magi.

Spiritual Warriors in the 2020's

"Live as if you expect your prayers to be answered." ~Edgar Cayce

The new decade and new year began with an inaugural ceremony for all our local newly elected and appointed officials on January 3rd. I was asked to present the closing blessing and excited to read the inspirational prayer that I had written. Dressed up in my black suit, sitting on stage in our Community Arts Center next to all the judges, politicians, and other officials, listening to the swearing in ceremony and guest speaker.

Towards the end of the event, about a dozen protesters in wheelchairs began chanting, "We Want Access Now" for a steady 20 minutes, referring to the lack of wheelchair access to City Hall. They did not stop when it was time for my Closing Prayer, so I spoke slowly into the microphone saying, "It is hard to get our work done with all the interruptions, until we realize the interruptions are our work." Everyone applauded.

It felt significant to begin this new decade with a prayer, "As you embark on your new positions with clear 20/20 vision, may you accept these words as a blessing;" Everyone said I did a good job, that my words were very meaningful, especially under the circumstances, and impactful because everyone was really listening. A few friends called me later to praise my leadership, inspiration, and holding the energy. Blessed be!

We felt that we were indeed holding sacred space for the new paradigm aligned with love that we all have been praying for. David and I felt like we were in a bubble of grace, in love with our new puppy, when news of the corona virus brought daily headlines in mid-March. People were being told to self-quarantine, as events were being canceled; schools, 'non-essential' businesses like restaurants, bars, shops, were all closing.

When a friend asked me for my point of view about this covid-19 situation, I sent an email to a group of friends and family. While usually refraining from controversy, this was an opportunity to expose the criminal syndicates that manipulate humanity behind the scenes, the insidious network of the Deep State, with agenda 21 and agenda 30. Looking at these nefarious agendas together is the way we reveal what has been hidden, so that we can blow their cover, and change the outcome. The following is a summation of the information that is a result of our research.

There is a world-wide psy-op (psychological operation) going on in a silent, spiritual war for the consciousness of humanity. This includes an insurrection and infiltration occurring at the highest levels of power in our world, not only in America. The global elite and disease profiteers have long had eugenics and population reduction as their goal. It is the big end game scenario to divide and conquer the people, control the masses through submission to tyranny, and turn humanity into an A.I. slave race.

There is much more to the corona virus than we were told by the deep state controlled main stream media. The media was banning anyone who challenged the COVID-19 narrative (Certificate Of Vaccination I.D.) Doctors were being silenced, attacked, and dis-credited. Statistics were being manipulated. COVID-19 tests were often ineffective, made false positives, or at worse, were contaminated with the actual virus.

All of these pandemics have been man made, bio engineered in labs, and patented. The patent is owned by Bill Gates, patent 060606. His vaccines have killed more children in Africa than the diseases they targeted. He is openly supporting forced vaccines and pushing mandated medicine. The release of this current virus was part of their socially engineered agenda to promote fear, social unrest, chaos, manipulate economies, false flag operations, push mandated medicine, and world genocide.

The problem-reaction-solution program equates with #1. Release a 'deadly' virus #2. Make people fearful and asking the authorities for help #3. Produce the solution in the form of an experimental vaccine that manipulates human DNA, and can cause adverse reactions. Why were remedies like Hydroxychloroquine, Ivermectin, and clorine-dioxide being banned? Why is there always another vaccine or booster required?

The mandatory mask mandate orders put out by the State governors were not backed by any legitimate law. The mask does little to prevent the spread of a virus. Even Dr. Fauci and the CDC said the masks are ineffective. Also, they can create secondary infection of bacterial pneumonia. Masks are being used to get people to conform and submit to authority, block our freedom of speech, and our ability to breathe.

The lockdowns are another form of authoritarian control, of giving our power away to a false narrative, tricking us into consenting to whatever 'they' tell us to do. Social distancing was another way to keep us away from one another and in fear of being contagious. Documentaries such as *Plandemic*, *The Real Anthony Fauci by Robert F. Kennedy* and friends, and *Fall Cabal Corona Virus Series* provide factual information about these agendas to do your own research.

Of all the commentaries on the pandemic, this synopsis from G.Edward Griffin is my favorite, which he titled, The Emperor Has No Clothes;

"Everyone by now is aware that the official narrative of COVID-19 is loaded with contradictions and fraud, but if the underlying concept, itself, the assertion that a deadly virus is stalking the human race, is not true, then we are facing something far more serious than bad science, poor judgment, and profiteering. If the contradictions and fraud are necessary to perpetuate a grand deception, then our response changes drastically. It changes because we are no longer engaged in a debate over the best way to cope with a global pandemic, but in resisting a propaganda campaign to maneuver us into passively accepting a new normal of servitude to a global technocratic dictatorship."

In my opinion, the biggest obstacle to arresting the global elite responsible for crimes against humanity is the ability of the people to realize who these criminals are and why they need to be arrested. Many people think this is inconceivable, unbelievable, and so out of their frame of reference that they go into cognitive dissonance or argue in defense of the very propaganda that has been socially engineered to control us.

We were meeting with so much resistance and denial when discussing these ideas with friends and family, that we had to agree to disagree, and avoid arguing. It was clear that these disagreements played into the divide and conquer agenda. So much controversy about if you were vaxxed or unvaxxed, masked or unmasked, social distancing and self quarantining or putting others at risk. Not to mention different political points of view.

As an answer to prayers for help, I was led to connect with several sister priestesses online, seers with whom there was a mutual resonance. "Return of the Priestess and the Rise of the Divine Feminine" introduced me to a group of inspiring spiritual women teachers. "Seven Sisters Mystery School; Restoring the Ancient Way of the Priestess" took me on a meaningful journey with the class, "Mother Mary Mystery Teachings."

In the Spring of 2020, my refuge was a deep dive into the Divine Feminine, specifically deepening my relationship with Mother Mary. I was given the assignment to commune with her for guidance and create a new website called, "Conversations With Mary." This brought me so much peace and joy that lifted my frequency to new heights. Continuing my studies with the "Holy Womb Chakra" mysteries led to new spiritual practices of daily mantras and yantras, as well as a new friendship with my teacher. It was a blessed time that has extended into the present time, strengthening my resolve as a Spiritual Warrior.

We were aware of the escalation of worldly events, the disinformation and false flag events that were engineered to produce more fear and distractions. The televised murder of George Floyd was an example, with the goal of creating a race war. Black Lives Matter is a Zionist organization funded by George Soros, with members trained as Marxists to occupy the USA, violently destroying property, while claiming to be peaceful protesters. The agenda to defund the police was a means to allow this insurgency to take down America. George Soros was filmed saying that Blacks are the easiest to manipulate, so this race war was being used as a distraction to create chaos.

Most of this engineered mayhem was to get Trump out of the White House with the upcoming election in November. Whether you like Trump or hate him, he is not part of the Deep State/Cabal, and has a plan to "drain the swamp" of corruption at the highest levels of power in our government, media, entertainment, science, health, banking, and corporate elites. The depth and extent of this corruption is far more than we realize.

While the evidence to take down this Deep State/Cabal has been available for years, it is the people that needed to be convinced. What has been unfolding is a slow disclosure of information to help dissolve the mind programming inflicted on the public. If Trump and the White Hats started arresting Deep State actors en masse, the media would call it a coup for a Trump dictatorship, and the socially engineered public would believe it.

The media began rigging the election by slanting the polling towards Joe Biden, while neglecting to present honest journalism on him, Hunter Biden, and first hand accounts of their schemes with China and Ukraine. They supported the suppression of free speech from opposing views with censorship on Twitter, Facebook, and YouTube. They hid Trumps accomplishments and promoted fake news about the Russian collusion hoax, which has now been validated through the release of the Twitter files.

The 2020 election was an illustration of widespread voter fraud, electronic theft, ballot stuffing, and destroying ballots. Trump won in a landslide, and yet on Nov. 9, the mainstream media declared Joe Biden/Kamala Harris the winners. Dominion voting machines deleted 2.7 million Trump votes, with over 450,000 Biden ballets mysteriously appearing overnight through illegal ballot stuffing as shown in the documentary, *2000 Mules*. Attorney Sydney Powell and General Mike Flynn have said they have conclusive, hard evidence of election fraud, and foreign interference in our election, which will soon be made public. In the meantime, allowing the Biden presidency, may be part of a positive psychological playbook, a public reeducation campaign to expose tyranny.

The battle is not between republicans and democrats, but a fight between those that want to free us and those that want to enslave us. The Global Elite plan to take down America, centralizing the power among a few wealthy narcissists. Trump stands between the American people and their goal of world domination. They want to eradicate the Constitution, Bill of Rights, and our freedoms. Our rights that protect us from enemies, foreign and domestic.

Trump has also been exposing the criminal networks of drug and child trafficking and pedophilia rings that are rampant among elite Satanic and Luciferian cults. Military soldiers were rescuing abused children from underground bases, many of which were destroyed during the Trump administration. This is all part of an ongoing silent, spiritual, global war between good and evil that has been going on behind the scenes.

Some of the disclosures that we saw publicly in 2022 include; the Jeffery Epstein and Ghisline Maxwell arrests exposing child trafficking and pedophilia rings; Hunter Biden's hard drives exposing his pedophilia as well as his treasonous interactions with China; The infiltration of the Chinese Communist Party in big tech, media, vaccine industry, and Dominion Voting Systems; the invasion at our southern borders by huge numbers of immigrants that the Biden administration are transporting all over the country and giving them welfare; Rand Paul called out Fauci and Gates for funding the Wuhan labs and gain of function research, as well as, for creating and patenting the COVID-19 virus; The food shortages are being engineered, as over 100 American food production plants have been destroyed; Chemtrails have been sprayed from airplanes for years containing aluminum, barium, cadmium, nanotechnology smart dust, and other toxins; Our foods are genetically modified and poisoned, the neurotoxin fluoride is in our drinking water, and people are dying from pharmaceuticals; Bill Gates is buying up American farmland; The normalization of sexual perversion, especially among young children, allowing them to make surgical sex changes without parental consent.

As 2023 arrived, more of the hidden agendas were revealed to the public; the silent disinformation war erupted into on the ground fighting in Ukraine and Russia, that could escalate into World War III, using the divide and conquer methods between nations, with propaganda for profit and distraction; The World Economic Forum rolled out their elitist, global tyranny plans with Klaus Schwab's Great Reset, aka. ,The Fourth Turning/Fourth Industrial Revolution, which looks like a continuation of Hitler's plan, the Fourth Reich; The engineering of a technological A.I. take over of humanity known as Transhumanism to control the world populations; Plans to crash the economy to implement a social credit score, with a central bank digital currency; False scientific information about "climate change," as an excuse to take away more of our freedoms and increase energy prices at the risk of millions of lives, all with the misdirected claim of "saving the planet;" Producing more virus variants and vaccinations for another engineered pandemic, to enforce medical tyranny, reduce more of the population, with mandated injections that have caused extensive injuries, including the "sudden death syndrome."

How do we awaken otherwise rational people from the mass hypnosis psychosis that has made an "incredulity barrier," which prevents them from seeing what is right in their face? Crimes against humanity have been happening and we need to pay attention. We need to connect the dots. The corporate media is the mouthpiece for the Global Elite and their control over the public's psyche is dependent on their dark agendas remaining concealed. This conflict will be resolved when enough of the people get the big picture and see how we have been socially engineered for generations.

Medical tyranny is the ultimate plan to take out dissent from the authoritarian agenda know as Agenda 21. COVID-19 is the culmination of the social engineering of our lives. David and I trust in our natural immunity and take supplements to keep us healthy and do not want the RMNA vaccine. David's Mother has allergies to medicines and vaccinations could make her sick or be potentially life threatening. When my family were getting vaccinations, I prayed to Mother Mary for protection and she said, "Don't worry, I've got this." And I believe her and that our loved ones are all safe.

In our personal lives, David was burned out from his job after six years of being with the Biocharger company. He was conflicted and struggling over his decision, when a series of events unfolded to let him know that it was time for him to leave by the end of February 2021. We moved out of our studio at the Pajama Factory in August because that had run its course after three years. We were feeling the changes.

We set up our Schweitzer Formula office back at home. It was a welcome change to work from home and simplify our life. Completing some home improvements, making raised bed vegetable gardens, and walking Magi kept us grounded, while we enjoyed some good rest and relaxation in our hammock. In the midst of all the worldly strife, we both said that we felt it was the happiest time of our lives. Our hearts were full.

We have been guided all long by the wisdom that reminds us that "there is a spiritual solution to every problem" (thank you Wayne Dyer). A Course in Miracles reminds us to "stay above the battleground," "there is no order of difficulty in miracles," and that "A happy outcome to all things is sure." We can wholeheartedly trust in God and know that the prayers of our heart are heard.

We all chose to be here at this worldwide awakening to the human shadow. If we are afraid of or angry at the cabal, we make it stronger. We can transcend their agendas by loving instead of getting angry. If humanity can move out of fear, raise our vibration, trust our intuition, and let go and let God work miracles through us, there is nothing we cannot do. If enough people felt loving for one day, it would overcome all fear.

We the people, with eyes to see, need to stand in our sovereignty and be willing to say that we do not acquiesce, and we do not consent to the lies, manipulations, corruption, and crimes against humanity, which are violations to natural law. We need to unite in our common purpose and know we are all in this together. "Where We Go One We Go All." United We Stand, divided we fall. Lets Rise Together in the United States of Grace!

In looking at the recent timeline, beginning with the COVID -20"19," we can see in 20/"20" hindsight, the nefarious Agenda 20/"21," that has led to a Catch 20/"22" situation. While it seems that we are trapped in a paradoxical problem where all is lost, in the story of the Hero's journey, this is exactly when things always work out! We can trust that we are all here in the Divine Orchestration and we will each play our part perfectly!

The benefits of the radical changes that came in with the 2020's is that it has prompted everyone to make a choice of love or fear and to be the light that overcomes darkness. As Swami Beyondananda says;

"We are in the transitional stage between the Age of Nefarious and the Age of Aquarius; It is called the Age of Hilarious. This is where we laugh because there is definitely something funny going on."

The good news is there has been a long-standing plan in effect to take down the cabal and we are actually winning the war against humanity. The "White Hats" are composed of all the Spiritual Warriors all over the world who have chosen to incarnate at this time of The Great Awakening, The Great Shift of the Ages, and Ascension Timeline. We are each here to be instruments of Divine Love, Light, and Peace.

While the battle between principalities is underway, the 5D consciousness can anchor love, forgiveness, and unity consciousness for the highest good of us all. As we regain our sovereignty, and withdrawal our consent from the lies and manipulations of social engineering, we will bring about the new paradigm aligned with love. If the script is already written with the victory of the light and positive timeline for humanity, then we can hold the vision of a happy outcome.

Once we have shifted our frame of reference from the fearful paradigm of the ego world, we can see that none of this is the ultimate reality of what is going on. Since problems are not solved at the level that they were created, we have to go to a transcendent level, to the oneness beyond duality. Damnation and Salvation are available to us all and we must each choose our destiny.

Due to this extreme polarization, this is a most significant time of great benefit and blessing, like a graduation from the mystery school. We can choose freedom from the ego and Identify with the absolute non-duality of Pure Spirit. Forgiveness of our illusions and accepting God's Plan for our salvation is our liberation and awakening. Now we can recognize the Truth of Who We Are and that...
One Loving Life Is All There Is.

Epilogue

"Forgiveness recognizes what you thought your brother did to you has not occurred. It does not pardon sins and make them real. It sees there was no sin. And in that view are all your sins forgiven." ~A Course In Miracles W-pII 1.1 1-3

A Course In Miracles, which has been my spiritual path for most of my life, puts everything in the proper perspective. Its theology teaches that the Truth of our Being is Eternal Spirit, as God Created us. We are having a dream that we have a separate identity, an ego self that we made, instead of the True Self that God Created.

Once we chose to believe that the separation was real, our decision-making mind identified with the ego, along with its insane thoughts of sin, guilt, fear, pain, and death, and special relationships. When we awaken from the dream and recognize our identity with the Holy Spirit, we experience the opposite: sane thoughts of the miracle, peace, forgiveness, and the holy relationship.

Both thought systems are given "life" by our belief in them by our decision-making minds having chosen them. We have to first recognize the power of our mind to mis-create that gave our power away to the ego's lies and illusory world. To regain our awareness of the minds power to create, through forgiveness, we will remember that we remain in the Heaven that we never left.

Once we chose the ego and identified with its dark thoughts, our separated self became that darkness. The ego is like the devil, which is only the part of our mind that chose to identify with the thought of separation. Having given away our power to the ego, we made a prison in the devil's illusory world of darkness, where we felt powerless to escape. While seemingly powerful in the dream, the ego disappears in the light of truth;

> "The "devil" is a frightening concept because he seems to be extremely powerful and extremely active. He is perceived as a force in combat with God, battling Him for possession of His creations. The devil deceives by lies, and builds kingdoms in which everything is in direct opposition to God. Yet he attracts men rather than repels them, and they are willing to "sell" him their souls in return for gifts of no real worth. This makes absolutely no sense...The mind can make the belief in separation very real and very fearful, and this belief is the "devil." It is powerful, active, destructive and clearly in opposition to God, because it literally denies His Fatherhood. Look at your life and see what the devil has made. But realize that this making will surely dissolve in the light of truth, because its foundation is a lie." ~A Course In Miracles T.3 VII.2:4-8; 5:1-4

Since the Holy Spirit is also in our mind, we can choose to have the errors of the ego be undone. In looking at our ego with the Holy Spirit, we look without judgment, and this is the meaning of forgiveness. Since the separation from God never occurred, the ego is really nothing, and our errors never occurred. As we begin to forgive and willingly look within our mind, our guilt over believing we separated, begins to be undone.

The identity that we perceived to be our self and our life in the ego's thought system of darkness, also begins to be undone. The more we choose the Holy Spirit instead of the ego, returning to our decision-making mind, we become an observer instead of a participant in the ego's dream. As we dis-identify with the ego, watching what we do, we will realize that the thought system that we once believed in, is not who we really are.

Within the illusion, we are free to believe that we made ourselves and our reality, but that will never make it true. Our minds are very powerful, but not to the extent that we can make illusions real. We think we can deny the truth, yet this does not mean that we have actually done so. When we awaken from the dream, which forgiveness helps us do, we will be happy to accept the fact that we made this all up.

"The world can teach no images of you unless you want to learn them. There will come a time when images have all gone by, and you will see you know not what you are. It is to this unsealed and open mind that truth returns, unhindered and unbound. Where concepts of the self have been laid by is truth revealed exactly as it is. When every concept has been raised to doubt and question, and been recognized as made on no assumptions that would stand the light, then is truth left free to enter in its sanctuary, clean and free of guilt. There is no statement that the world is more afraid to hear than this: I do not know the thing I am, and therefore do not know what I am doing, where I am, or how to look upon the world or myself. Yet in this learning is salvation born. And What you are will tell you of Itself." ~A Course In Miracles T.31 V. 17

A Course In Miracles dovetails with other non-dualistic thought systems that have the objective of Self-Realization. It does not fall into the category of "spiritual side-stepping" in that it states our first steps involve looking at the horror of the ego thought system with the Holy Spirit. In looking, without judgment, the miracle occurs through bringing the darkness to the light, where true healing and transformation occurs.

Quantum Physics scientific research has come to the same realization through the concept that we affect the quantum field by our observation of it. The concept of the holographic universe also illustrates our oneness, interconnectedness, and the cause and effect principles of the infinite order. It can prove that matter is an illusion, and everything is really light (energy) and sound (frequency).

Why should we be surprised to see the world the ego made is an inversion of the truth? An upside down perception. Can we open our minds with the willingness to question everything we think we believe? We have been down the rabbit hole for a long time, now it is time to turn around and go up into the light! We are here to be the "light," expressing that good energy and "sound" the trumpet, to lift the frequency!

Our one problem was forgetting and that made us fearful. Humanity has been lulled into the manipulation of our perception, locking us into a prison of our five senses. As we disconnect from "the matrix," we will no longer identify with the polarity that the matrix depends on to control us. Once we wake up and become aware of the game, we free our minds, and the game is over.

Our one answer is remembering that we have been having a silly dream, and that we can become lucid dreamers. We can identify with our Infinite Being of Love; Oneness in awareness of Itself; Free, Sovereign, Whole, Divine Beings. We remain as God Created Us, and that is True for All of Us, because We are All in this Together. Oneness, not division, is the path to freedom.

Fighting makes division. To fight for freedom is an oxymoron. There is no need to fight to be right, but there is a need to do what is right for you. We exercise our freedom by making choices, freedom to say "no" when necessary. We demonstrate our sovereignty with peaceful non-compliance. We release trying to change people or situations, we just express our natural empowerment and authenticity.

When we try to define ourselves, we limit what is limitless. We are so much more than we have been socially engineered to believe. We are not who we think we are; not our past, our personality, our body/brain complex, our accomplishments. Can we let it all go and be comfortable not knowing? In the spirit of limitless possibilities, here is a vision of our unlimited potential called, "The Big Idea;"

If the collective consciousness of humanity is like imaginal cells in a chrysalis, what is the big idea that makes us transform into a butterfly? What if a sinister force was trying to kill off humanity, and like the caterpillar going into metamorphosis, it thinks it is the end of the world. Then the caterpillar wakes up and remembers the power of its mind and says "no," I am not going to do that. I am not going to die, I am really going to live! I am going to remember the Divine Love within me, the spiritual truth that I am a Divine Being that is under no laws but Gods.

If anything is possible and miracles occur naturally as expressions of love, imagine that humanity chooses to bust out of the matrix or cocoon, or whatever limitations, and chooses to be free. Chooses to live in love, truth, peace, prosperity. Chooses to trust that fear and evil have no power to hurt us, that we are safe and healed and whole. Like the ugly duckling becoming a swan and a caterpillar becoming a beautiful butterfly, humanity emerges from its near death experience and lifts up with wings that transcend fear and death by embodying Love and Life.
So Be It and So It Is.

How do we get there? By being the miraculous Power of Love. The heart is the great transformer. Take a deep breath and imagine what it feels like to be in your heart. Feel the emotion of gratitude, feel grateful for the love within you, for your life here and now. Take another breath and remember that we are an eternal soul, a spiritual being, created in the image of our Divine Creator. Our spirit is in a state of grace forever. Since we shape our experience by our thoughts, we can envision so much love and positive energy well up in humanity that we bust out in light and laughter! We overcome gravity with levity as we choose to be loving and happy. It's contagious! Spread de-light and let love lift us up together.

There is no end to Our One Loving Life.

Don't miss out!

Visit the website below and you can sign up to receive emails whenever Mary Woods publishes a new book. There's no charge and no obligation.

https://books2read.com/r/B-A-GFUW-VKFFC

BOOKS2READ

Connecting independent readers to independent writers.